Mom, Will This Chicken Give Me Man Boobs?

. . .

My Confused, Guilt-Ridden,

and Stressful Struggle to Raise

A GREEN FAMILY

Robyn Harding

MOM, WILL THIS CHICKEN GIVE ME MAN BOOBS?

GREYSTONE BOOKS

D&M PUBLISHERS INC.

Vancouver/Toronto/Berkeley

Greystone Books
A division of D&M Publishers Inc.
2323 Quebec Street, Suite 201
Vancouver BC Canada V5T 4S7
www.greystonebooks.com

Library and Archives Canada Cataloguing in Publication
Harding, Robyn
Mom, will this chicken give me man boobs? : my confused, guilt-ridden,
and stressful struggle to raise a green family / Robyn Harding.

ISBN 978-1-55365-390-5

1. Sustainable living—Humor. 2. Environmental protection—Humor.
3. Suburban life—Humor. I. Title.

PN6231.E66H37 2009   640   C2008-906170-5

Editing by Susan Folkins
Copy editing by Eve Rickert
Cover illustration by Laura Kinder
Printed and bound in Canada by Friesens
Printed on acid-free paper that is forest friendly (100% post-consumer recycled paper)
and has been processed chlorine free.
Distributed in the U.S. by Publishers Group West

We gratefully acknowledge the financial support of the Canada Council for the
Arts, the British Columbia Arts Council, the Province of British Columbia through
the Book Publishing Tax Credit, and the Government of Canada through the Book
Publishing Industry Development Program (BPIDP) for our publishing activities.

Acknowledgments

THANK YOU TO: my publisher, Rob Sanders, for his support and patience with this project; my editor, Susan Folkins, for turning my endless ramblings into a story; to my neighbors in Kitsilano, for their guidance and inspiration; and to my family, for being such good sports.

Contents

• • •

Prologue

• • •

IT WASN'T AN overnight decision. It was more of a gradual awakening spurred on by intense media coverage and some neighborhood peer pressure. The planet was in a perilous state. Human beings had been destroying the earth for centuries, and it was time we stopped. But we couldn't just stop! We had to repair the years and years of damage we'd done. It was up to us to save the planet for our children... and our children's children... and our children's children's children... And I was going to be one of those conscientious people who made a difference. One day, my great-great-great-grandchildren would thank me for saving the world for them.

I had always admired people like Al Gore, who made enlightening documentaries, and Sheryl Crow, whose biodiesel tour bus was full of recycled toilet paper. I thought it was great that celebrities like Leonardo DiCaprio were hanging out in the Arctic, making films about global warming and endangered polar bears. These people set the environmental bar a little high, but I wasn't going to be intimidated. I wanted to jump on that green bandwagon. I wanted to put solar panels on my roof and feed my vegetable waste to a bucketful of worms that lived under my sink. I wanted to wear only organic cotton clothing and deodorant made from salt crystals. And I was going to do it. I was going green!

And then reality struck. I discovered that being environmentally friendly is hard. And expensive! And where do you draw the line? How far do you go? Isn't it tough enough raising a family these days without feeling guilty every time you get in your car? Or turn up the heat? Or give your kid a banana from Ecuador? I'm telling you that it is.

Our mothers had it easy. They didn't have to choose between organic or conventional produce. They didn't have to worry about using plastic wrap or harsh chemical cleaners or whether that chocolate bar was fair-trade. No one used to ask if your kid's T-shirt was made by child labor. Of course it was! In some countries, kids had to have jobs.

I'm sure our mothers had their own worries, but being a parent today has got to be about a thousand times harder. And more stressful. And infinitely more confusing! We're faced with so many choices affecting our children's health and that of the planet that it boggles the mind. Should we get a biodiesel car, or are crops grown for biofuels destroying our forests? Should we be eating organic meat or is free-range okay? What? Free-range is not a government regulated label, so it could mean basically nothing? Great. Oh, and don't be fooled by terms like "natural" and "green" either. They're just marketing gimmicks designed to *trick* you into thinking that a product is healthy or good for the environment, when it's probably not.

And what about the mixed messages we receive? The spotty information? Organic is good—but it has to be *certified* organic or don't bother. Eating local is more important, anyway—though you really should be calculating food miles to ensure that the local tomato you just purchased is better than an efficiently shipped one from California. Microwave ovens are bad for the environment. Wait! They're actually more energy efficient than regular ones. Dishwashers use too much water and energy. No, they actually use half the energy and one-sixth of the water used in handwashing. It's enough to drive a person to drink (there are organic wines available, but they're really expensive).

Of course, we need to enrich our children's lives, too. The world is becoming an increasingly competitive place. But in this day and age, we're forced to consider the environmental impact of all their extracurricular activities. While I've tried to choose programs in my neighborhood, I still have to drive my daughter, Tegan, to her dance classes. The dance studio's not that far away, but it's not that close, either. My husband, John, coaches our son, Ethan's, rugby team. They usually drive to practices (that are very nearby) and games (that are not so nearby). I want my kids to be healthy, active, well-rounded individuals, but what about the emissions? What good is being healthy, active, and well-rounded if the ice caps melt and your house is under water?

At least I'm teaching them to swim—and the swimming pool where they take their lessons is just down the street. But I recently read that swimming pools are terrible for the environment. It takes significant power to heat them, they use too much water, and the chlorine in them can form toxic chemicals when mixed with dirt or leaves or even dead skin cells. So my kids are splashing around in a greenhouse gas–emitting, carcinogenic soup. But what's the alternative? They don't learn to swim? What if the ice caps do melt and there's a flood? Or a tsunami? The image haunts me: My kids flailing helplessly in the water, yelling, "If only my mom wasn't so goddamn green!" just before they go under.

So if I wanted to be an environmentally conscious parent, what was I supposed to do with my kids? Sit at home and play secondhand board games by candlelight? Haul them to dance class and soccer practice by bike trailer? And what was I supposed to feed them—carrots grown in my own garden and milk from the pet goat that lived in the backyard? Was I supposed to humanely slaughter my own grass-fed pet cow? Catch wild salmon with a homemade fishing line and barbless hook?

And what about when special occasions rolled around? Did I have to throw a stimulating and entertaining eighth birthday party without producing any waste? Wasn't the Christmas season stressful enough without worrying about doing it up green? What about spring break? And summer holidays? God forbid our vacation produced any emissions!

So maybe it was just too much to ask a parent to care about the environment. But it couldn't be. How could I look my kids in the eye if I didn't care about the future of the planet? I watched *An Inconvenient Truth*, Al Gore's documentary about global warming. I knew what was going to happen if we didn't do something! But was it possible to raise my family green and still hold onto my sanity? Well, that remained to be seen.

I vowed to try, though. Because I wanted to be that sustainable, low-impact, green mom, I really did. Despite the guilt, the confusion, and the stress, I felt compelled to whittle my carbon footprint down to an itty-bitty size two. But could I do it? Was it even possible? And was I really willing to go the distance?

This book describes my valiant efforts to become an enviro-mom: the dark-forest-green highs, the pale-mint lows, and the chartreuse in-betweens. It is the story of one woman's struggle to juggle motherhood, a career, and a commitment to the planet . . . and to keep from losing her mind.

Pale Mint

• • •

REMEMBER (RATHER FONDLY) a time when we didn't have to think about the environment. When I was a kid, no one knew that we were wrecking the planet. It was the seventies. Our parents tossed us in the backseat of the gas-guzzling station wagon with nary a second thought (or a seatbelt for that matter). They fed us oranges from Florida and apples from New Zealand, all liberally sprayed with pesticides. We scarfed down prepackaged meats like bologna and mock-chicken loaf. We didn't even know what animal we were eating, let alone whether that animal had access to outdoor pastures and was treated with antibiotics. I ate raw wieners. I loved individually wrapped processed-cheese slices!

I grew up in Quesnel, a small city in the interior of British Columbia. Quesnel is a logging town, home to a number of sawmills and pulp and paper mills. Obviously, when you live in a city where most of the population makes a living from killing trees, you don't spend a lot of time calculating your carbon footprint. When I was a teenager, I got a summer job at a gas station. Everyday, I pumped pickup trucks full of leaded gasoline so their drivers could go to the forest and chop down some conifers. Though I was blissfully unaware, I wasn't off to a very good environmental start.

But my parents were nature-lovers. When I was young, we had a huge vegetable garden in our half-acre backyard. On weekends, we would go hiking or cross-country skiing or canoeing. We never had speedboats or snowmobiles like so many of our friends and neighbors. We weren't full-fledged hippies like the ones who sold honey (and probably pot) from the ramshackle hobby farm at the end of our road. But maybe this early appreciation of nature planted a tiny seed of environmentalism inside of me—it just took a very long time to grow.

In the late eighties, I moved to Vancouver to attend journalism school. Even before being green was "in," many people considered Vancouver a left-wing, tree-hugger's haven. "Granola eaters," they called us—and not really in a nice way. But other than a penchant for tie-dye, Birkenstocks, and marijuana smoking, I didn't really see that Vancouverites were a lot different from other city dwellers. I was just happy to be living in a larger center where people didn't wear so much plaid.

I settled into the first of the thirteen downtown apartments I would live in over the course of the next ten years. At this time, homeowners in Vancouver had blue boxes for recycling their plastics, glass, and paper. But as an apartment dweller, I wasn't given a recycling box. So just as I'd grown up doing, I tossed all that stuff in the trash without giving it a second thought. At least I recycled my pop cans and beer bottles—though that was strictly because I was broke and really needed the $3.50 I got for lugging them all to the bottle depot.

Over the next decade, the state of the environment became more of a public issue. There were rumblings about the hole in the ozone, endangered species, and overflowing landfills. Still, it wasn't the all-out media frenzy it is today. And though I wasn't overly concerned about it, I had begun to do my little environmental part. I worked in an office where I dutifully deposited my paper in the recycling box. (It was the least I could do after all those years spent in the tree-slaughter capital of the universe.) And I walked as much as possible. Apartment buildings had gotten blue boxes by then, so I was also taking care of my household recyclables.

But then, in 1998, John and I packed up our two-bedroom apartment, loaded eighteen-month-old Ethan into our Ford Escort, and moved to Calgary, Alberta. Calgary, Alberta—the Houston, Texas, of Canada. We were lured there by the promise of cheap real estate, low taxes, and high-paying jobs. From all over Canada, cool young families like ours were flocking to the Promised Land. It was going to be great. We'd have a big house! A big bank account! An SUV! Make that two! I chose to ignore the warnings about the nine months of winter and the conservative politics. "Don't be so negative," I would say, optimistically. "I won't care about that stuff. I'm going to be rich."

It actually worked out—for a while. We bought a big house. We didn't have two SUVs, but we did have a station wagon and a sedan. And we even had some money in the bank. I didn't realize that the nine months of winter and conservative politics would cause me to exist in a mildly depressed funk for a significant portion of our stay, but that's another story. And of course, the state of the environment was the last thing on our minds as we made our home in the oil-rich province.

My first job in Calgary was at a downtown advertising agency. When I moved into my new office, I found a computer, a desk, and a filing cabinet. Where was my recycling box? They must have forgotten to give me one. I decided to go see the office manager.

"We don't do that here," she croaked, lighting a cigarette. It's true. She *lit a cigarette.* The office policy did not provide recycling boxes, but it did allow smoking in the office (with its sealed windows) after regular office hours. So at four o'clock (regular office hours were from eight AM to four PM), the air conditioning would shut off, and the smokers would light up. It wasn't that bad, I told myself. I was making quite a bit more money than I did in Vancouver. And I only had to breathe the secondhand smoke for about an hour and a half each day, so that was probably the equivalent of smoking, I don't know, three or four cigarettes?

That job didn't last long. After seven months (which felt like seventeen years), I left to do some freelance writing. And I wanted to have another baby. I knew I couldn't get pregnant while I was working at the smoke-bubble agency. It was one thing for me to inadvertently smoke three ciggies a day, but quite another for my fetus. So I resigned and quickly got myself knocked up. On February 29, 2000, Tegan was born, with very pink lungs.

By this time, I was starting to hear the terms "global warming" and "climate change" on the news, but I wasn't paying much attention. I was an Albertan now. Our province just kept getting richer and richer off of oil and gas. I didn't have to bother myself with the state of the planet. And I had babies! I was stressed-out, sleep-deprived, and caught in the endless cycle of motherhood: feed them, then clean up; feed them, then clean up; wait for them to poop, then clean up; feed them, then clean up . . . I was too exhausted to think about global warming.

I admit it, I used disposable diapers. But what were my options? Cloth diapers? Get real. I didn't have the wherewithal to be dumping poop into the toilet and then soaking diapers in a bucket before washing, drying, and folding them. It was too much. There were diaper services to do the work for you, but I was on maternity leave. I couldn't afford that.

It was at a friend's baby shower that I heard of another alternative. A pretty Asian woman I had not met before mentioned that her child was already potty-trained.

"Wow," I said, "How old is he?"

"Three months," she replied, rather smugly.

"I—I don't understand. Can he crawl to the toilet already?"

"You just have to be in tune with your child's bowel rhythms and prepared to respond to them," she explained.

If it meant no more diapers, I could do that.

But upon further grilling, the woman admitted that potty training a three-month-old consisted of watching your baby like a hawk until he got a funny look on his face, then rushing to hold him over the toilet. That just wasn't for me. I had other things to do besides sitting around staring at my baby and waiting for her to make her "I'm about to take a crap" face.

I felt kind of bad that my kids' disposable diapers were going to sit in a landfill for all eternity, but no one really seemed to care that much at the time—at least they didn't in Calgary. Would I have changed my ways had I known that, according to Adria Vasil's 2007 book *Ecoholic*, the average baby contributes between five thousand and seven thousand diapers to landfills over the course of its diaper-wearing lifetime? It's hard to say. I was only getting five hours of sleep a night. If I'd been worrying about the environment too, I probably would have had a nervous breakdown.

The poor new mommies of today. Don't they have enough to worry about without thinking of the environment? I'm telling you, they do. Is the house sufficiently baby-proofed? Is the car seat installed properly? Is there lead paint on that choo-choo train? Is it bad if I have a beer when I'm nursing? Is nursing going to ruin my breasts forever?

A few months ago, I witnessed two new moms discussing the diaper dilemma. One said, "I just feel like cloth diapers are such a huge inconvenience. And what about all the hot water and soap used for washing? That's not great for the environment, either. I'll do my environmental part in other ways."

My mom, who also happened to be witnessing this exchange, chuckled. "I used cloth diapers for all three of my children, and I only had a wringer washing machine."

"True," I said, "but that was in the olden days. You had no choice." (My mom hates it when I call her era "the olden days." I'm starting to understand how she feels. About a month ago, Tegan asked me if *pens* had been invented when I was a kid.)

But that's enough about diapers. Besides, they're only part of the environmental carnage of the baby years. Babies require so much plastic! My kids drank out of plastic baby bottles (which are now sitting in a Calgary landfill, where they will leach their toxic chemicals into the soil for the next seven hundred years). And every child needs a car seat, a high chair, a bathtub ring, and a baby swing. And how can we expect them to develop normally without an exersaucer, a musical mobile, and nine thousand other educational plastic toys?

At least the environmental devastation of those trying years didn't last forever. Both my kids were potty-trained by the time they were two and a half. It wasn't three months, but I still thought it was pretty good. Soon, they were eating solid foods, so no more plastic baby bottles were required. I donated all of my baby appliances to a women's shelter, so at least they were being reused.

But then Ethan started kindergarten. Unlike some cities, Calgary does not require children to attend the public school located in their catchment area. This seemed to breed a mind-set that attending the school closest to you was *settling*. And I totally bought into it! Obviously, that school three blocks away was not good enough for my future genius. Anything that nearby had to be a cop-out. No, the elementary school five miles away would offer him a far superior education. My child deserved to attend the best school, not the most conveniently located one.

I guess it was a case of a first-time parent's insecurity and self-doubt. And I got caught up in the mommy peer pressure. Everyone I knew was sending their kids to French Immersion, an alternative school, a "charter" school, or Montessori. Those who could afford it put their kids in private school (though my egalitarian principles—not to mention my bank account—would not allow it). I knew parents who hadn't set foot inside a church since they were toddlers who were sending their kids to Catholic schools because they were better funded. The overwhelming message I received was that regular public school just didn't cut it anymore.

Growing up in Quesnel, I had attended Dragon Lake Elementary, a small public school located just down the street from me. Every morning, I walked to school with my friends. After school, we walked home together and then played around the neighborhood. It was all so easy, so convenient, so comforting . . . and I turned out all right, didn't I?

But what if my parents had made the extra effort? What if they had gotten up half an hour earlier, loaded my brothers and me into the car, and braved the ice and snow to take us to another school with a fancy creative writing program or more French classes? Perhaps then, I'd be writing award-winning literary fiction à la Margaret Atwood—when I wasn't chatting fluently to my sophisticated francophone friends. I decided I would make the sacrifice and send my son to the best school in the city, not the closest. The kid deserved a fighting chance.

, And so it was that every morning, I drove Ethan approximately four miles to school. Sure, it doesn't sound that far. But first, I had to corral Tegan, who was going through the horrible threes. (She was good when she was two, but on her third birthday she turned evil.)

"Time to go!" I'd say cheerfully, though I'm sure the fear was evident in my voice.

"I'm not going!" she would screech, and barricade herself in her room.

Ten minutes later, when I had cajoled/bribed/threatened her to emerge, we would don our winter coats, boots, hats, and mittens (well, we only had to do that for nine months of the year), pile into our station wagon, and set off.

At the risk of stereotyping an entire city, Calgarians are maniacs on the road. Okay, maybe it's because I drive like a ninety-year-old with trifocals, but the drivers in Calgary were so aggressive—and fast! Each morning as I merged onto Bow Trail (in keeping with the city's cowboy theme, these mini-autobahns go by the misnomer "trail"), I said a silent prayer. "Please let us not be crushed to death by one of the hundreds of Ford Expeditions, Toyota Tundras, or Mercedes SUVs bearing down on us at breakneck speed." In addition, the "trail" was covered in snow and ice (but only for nine months of the year), which increased the likelihood of being mowed down by an SUV careening out of control.

By the time we got to school, I was usually slicked with sweat and having trouble breathing. I would pull up behind the stream of idling SUVs and say a silent "thank you" that we had made it alive. The commute was stressful, dangerous, and expensive (I was burning through a tank of gas a week), not to mention terrible for the environment. But it would all be worth it when Ethan won the Nobel Peace Prize for curing prostate cancer.

So we made it through that first year of kindergarten. As we approached first grade, one of the super-moms said to me: "So, when Ethan is attending a full day, what will he do at lunchtime?"

What did she mean, "What will he do at lunchtime"? Why, he'd eat his sandwich, throw away his apple, and play with his friends on the monkey bars, of course. Wasn't that the whole point of lunchtime? To fuel up, burn off steam, and build friendships? Apparently not at this school.

Because Calgary public schools do not offer lunchtime supervision, parents must pay the out-of-school care provider for this service. It wasn't too expensive, and lunch-hour playtime is an integral part of developing kids' social IQs—or so I'd always thought. But it soon became apparent that only mothers who didn't really love their children left them at school over the lunch-hour.

At noon, the stream of SUVs would return, pick up the little darlings, and take them home for nourishing home-cooked meals and mommy-bonding time. Mothers who lived a little too far away packed a picnic lunch or took the kids out for a

Happy Meal. What happened to eating a crappy sandwich and running around with your friends for an hour? Apparently this too was a thing of the past.

The thought of Ethan standing on the playground with the other unloved children (in my mind's eye, they all looked like chimney sweeps) was too much for me. While our fifteen-minute commute made going home for lunch a little tight, I figured I could do it.

When Ethan went off to first grade, I told him I'd be picking him up at noon.

"Why?" he asked.

"Because I love you," I told him.

So, I pulled up to the school at exactly 11:58. "Get in!" I shrieked, as my son strolled casually to the car. "Hurry up! Move it! Let's go!"

"How was your morning?" I asked sweetly, as I raced along the highway, one eye glued to the dashboard clock.

"Fine," he replied.

"Great," I said. "That's great that your morning was . . . fine." If this was supposed to be quality bonding time, he was going to have to be a little more forthcoming.

When we pulled into our driveway, the dashboard clock read: 12:15. "How about a nourishing home-cooked can of ravioli?" I asked, helping the kids out of their booster seats and hurrying them toward the house.

At 12:30, I stood over Ethan, watching him eat. "Can you eat a little faster, honey?" (Since the whole point of coming home for lunch was mommy-bonding time, I refrained from yelling: "Eat faster goddammit! We're going to be late!") Finally, at 12:45, I dragged the kids back to the car, merged onto the "trail" and hurtled back to school. We made it, just in time. But I knew then that I'd never do it again. Yes, I would be shunned as one of those mothers who loved her children just a little bit less, but my nerves couldn't take the stress.

So there I was, driving back and forth to school each day. When Tegan started half-day preschool at the same school, I was doing it three times! Honestly, I didn't even think about the effect this was having on the environment. In the car-culture and oil-and-gas economy of Calgary, it didn't really come up in conversation. And I wasn't the worst offender. There were people who drove for forty minutes each way to send their children to this coveted school . . . in minivans and SUVs. For six to ten years! But thanks to my commitment to their education, my kids would probably grow up to invent a car that ran on grass clippings anyway.

Still, I wasn't *completely* oblivious of the environment during those Calgary years. I had been a diligent recycler in Vancouver, and I planned to continue in my new city. But though Vancouver implemented a curbside recycling program in 1990, Calgary still (as of 2008, at least) doesn't have one. What were we supposed to do with all our paper, glass, cans, and plastics? Well, we were supposed to drive our recyclable items to one of forty-nine recycling depots in the city. It was a pain in the ass, frankly, but John and I made a commitment to do it.

Unfortunately, finding the time to do it was not easy. With two young kids and our jobs, trips to the recycling depot were all too infrequent. I would wait until we were cowering in one room of the house, the rest taken over by the kids' art projects, magazines, and empty milk jugs. There we were, a normal family living like some crazy spinster with a houseful of newspapers and twenty-two cats! Finally, when I couldn't take it any more, we would load several large cardboard boxes to overflowing with newspapers, papers, plastic milk jugs, and ravioli cans and drive to the recycling depot at the strip mall. We stood in the frigid weather (only for nine months of the year, though) and deposited our recycling into the appropriate bin. Eventually, I caved in and paid a private company twelve bucks a month to pick up my recycling curbside. It seemed a small price to pay to keep from dropping dead of hypothermia at the strip mall's recycling depot.

That was another contributing factor to our negative environmental impact: the weather. As I may have mentioned, Calgary has a very long, very cold winter. Our heating costs were astronomical. When we first moved there, we were renting a drafty older home and paying up to four hundred dollars a month for heat! And Calgary's primary source of energy is coal. That was four hundred dollars' worth of dirty, polluting, non-renewable fossil fuels. Could I have made a greener choice? Yes. The electric company had an option for using wind power, but it cost a little more. I should have done it, but with my mind-set at the time I thought, "That sounds great, but with the money I have to pay to have my recycling picked up, I don't think I can afford it."

And I wasn't any better when it came to our diet. Eating locally produced food was a completely foreign concept at the time. Besides, what can grow in that climate? I'll tell you what: beef. (I did eat some pretty good steak during my stint as an Albertan.)

I was mildly concerned about pesticides and hormone use, though. I'll admit this was purely for health reasons. At the risk of sounding like a moron, it really hadn't occurred to me that traditional farming methods could be hazardous, not just to me and my family, but to the environment. I know it seems obvious that chemical pesticides and fertilizers are damaging to the land and waterways, but I was so preoccupied with the thought of the malignant tumors they could grow on my children's lymph nodes that I didn't really think about that side of it.

Organic food was not offered at any of my regular grocery stores, but I learned there was a natural-food store located downtown. I drove to check it out. While it was a little out of the way, I felt excited to be shopping for the healthiest food choices for my family. But the moment I set foot inside, it was apparent that the store was targeted to the city's hard-core hippies. Everyone looked so . . . well, dirty. And the staff were so intimidating. They all had multiple piercings and funky eyewear, and while they served me, they talked among themselves about indie bands and miso gravy. They sniffed condescendingly when I took out my leather wallet. They sneered at the brand of rice cakes I'd bought. They made me feel superficial and out of place. Plus, it was all way too expensive anyway.

I wish I could blame this less-than-green era of my life on Calgary. It's a fact (according to some Green Party literature recently dropped into my Vancouver mailbox) that Alberta is responsible for about one-third of Canada's total greenhouse gas emissions. I wish I could say I was kidnapped by some money-obsessed, J.R. Ewing–type oil barons who brainwashed me into their way of thinking. But I know the choices I made were my own.

While Calgary's sprawling layout and lack of curbside recycling made it a little harder to be green, I still could have made more of an effort. To be perfectly honest, I didn't care that much about the planet then. It pains me to admit it, but I didn't. I guess I was too selfish, too self-absorbed, and too busy raising my kids. Plus, I was waging a long and difficult battle with seasonal affective disorder (but only for nine months of the year).

At the time, I was satisfied with my level of greenness. I was pale, pale mint, and that was okay with me. But I wonder, sometimes, how green I would be if I had stayed there. When the global warming media frenzy hit, would I have moved my kids to the neighborhood school? Paid a little more for wind power? Or would I have used my money for vacations in Mexico and pushed global warming to the back of my mind? Because really, Calgary could stand to warm up a few degrees.

The Accidental
Environmentalist

• • •

J**UST IN CASE** we hadn't done enough damage to the
environment during our five-year stint in Calgary, we
decided to belch twenty-odd tons of carbon into
the atmosphere. Okay, we didn't *decide* to belch all that carbon
into the air, but unwittingly, we did. In 2003, we moved from
Calgary to Perth, Australia.

John is from Perth, and his entire family still lives there. We
decided to spend five years living in his hometown. The kids
and I would get to know John's family and learn about the culture and lifestyle of Australia. Plus, if I had had to endure one
more Calgary winter, I would surely have slit my wrists (I may
have mentioned that winter there is very long and very cold).

The environment was not exactly top-of-mind as we flew to
the other side of the planet. In fact, we didn't give our carbon

emissions a second thought. People weren't really talking about them then. Flying was still about fun and adventure, not melting ice caps and dead polar bears. Besides, we'd been so ensconced in the Alberta mentality of "black gold" that the pollution our flight was causing didn't even cross our minds.

When John and I first met in 1994, we weren't thinking about the environmental ramifications of our relationship. I guess it was a mistake falling for a guy from Western Australia, probably the farthest geographic point from Western Canada. I suppose one of us should have said, "I really like you but . . . I just think this relationship would create too many carbon emissions." But we were young and falling in love and drinking heavily at the time (more about that later). It just didn't occur to us.

So now that the damage was done, what were we supposed to do? Was John never supposed to see his family again? Were my kids never meant to meet their grandparents and cousins and aunts and uncles? To learn about their Aussie heritage? Was I supposed to just stay in Calgary until I killed myself from seasonal affective disorder?

We flew from Calgary to Vancouver and then on to L.A. Once again, the state of the planet was the farthest thing from our minds as we spent four days staying in a crappy Anaheim motel, eating overpriced meals out of styrofoam containers, and riding on energy-consuming roller coasters at Disneyland. Then it was a fourteen-hour overnight flight to Sydney. We spent a couple of weeks there, sightseeing and visiting friends, before renting a van and driving down the coast to Melbourne.

It was approximately 108 degrees Fahrenheit, so we blasted the air conditioner the whole way. We'd just come from a November in Calgary, for god's sake. We would have spontaneously combusted without the AC!

After touring around Melbourne, we drove back to Sydney and hopped another plane to Brisbane, where we rented another vehicle to travel the Sunshine Coast. Finally we drove back to Brisbane and flew across Australia to Perth. Environmentally speaking, we were off to a bad start. But little did I know that life in the Southern Hemisphere would automatically make us kinder to the planet.

In Perth, we rented a small, brick house in a quaint neighborhood a few miles from the Indian Ocean. It had a reticulated rose garden, a built-in barbecue, and air conditioning (a prerequisite for transitioning from a Calgary winter to a Perth summer). It would have been great if not for the cockroach infestation.

The bugs were like something from a horror movie! They were the size of mice and had tails like little vermin helicopters. Ethan's bedroom was adjacent to the back garden, so he got the worst of it. One night, I was awoken by a bloodcurdling scream coming from my six-year-old son. I flew out of bed and met him in the hallway. "It ran across my l-lip!" he stammered, tears streaming down his face. "M-my lip!"

"Oh my god!" I cried. "Come sleep in my bed. Dad can go sleep with the cockroaches since they are his native insects and it was his bright idea to move here anyway." (Or something snarky like that.)

A few days later, after Tegan found a dead cockroach in Barbie's suv, we called the exterminator. I didn't like the idea of our home being sprayed with chemicals. It had to be bad for our health and was probably bad for the environment too. But we just couldn't live on edge like that. The tension was affecting our marriage. Every time I spotted a piece of dryer lint on the floor, I would scream hysterically and do the heebie-jeebie dance. John would come running.

"What? What?"

"Nothing," I'd say sheepishly. "I thought it was a cockroach, but it's just fluff."

"You scared the crap out of me."

"Sorry."

One evening, I opened the cupboard below the sink to put something in the garbage. A cockroach scurried out and ran across my bare foot.

"Ahhhhhhhhhhhhhhh!" I screamed. Then one more time, just for the hell of it. "Ahhhhhhhhhhhhhhhhhhhhhhhhhhhh!"

John was there in seconds. "Oh my god! What?"

"A c-c-cockroach! For real this time!"

He was not sympathetic. "Christ! You screamed like a severed head had just rolled out of the cupboard."

"Well, sooooorry!" I snapped. "Maybe I'm not used to cohabiting with enormous, germ-covered insects that can survive a nuclear blast and live for two weeks with their heads cut off!" (Or something snarky like that.)

When the exterminator came (the first time), he reassured me. "The chemicals we use nowadays are so safe that we don't even wear protective equipment."

"That's good," I said, breathing a sigh of relief.

"Yeah," he replied, "but they rarely kill the cockroaches."

"What?" I screeched. "Can't you get some of those highly toxic, dangerous chemicals on the black market or something? I want those suckers dead!"

Obviously, this was not a very environmentally friendly stance, but I was having anxiety attacks! I was taking valerian and Saint-John's-wort to try to soothe my frazzled nerves. Unfortunately, our exterminator lacked the appropriate connections to get his hands on the deadly poisons of old, but, by the second spraying, the cockroach onslaught had slowed to a trickle.

Yes, we were living in a house liberally sprayed with (mildly) toxic chemicals. Yes, we had contributed significant airplane emissions in our move abroad, but in other ways, we were starting to be quite good to the planet. While I often tease my husband that Western Australia is ten years behind North America technologically and in gender roles ("Get me a beer, Sheila, while I dial up the Internet!"), it was far ahead of Alberta in environmental awareness. It only makes sense that Aussies would be concerned about global warming. They simply can't get much hotter without cooking to death.

Each house in Perth was provided with three wheelie-bins: one for glass, plastic, and paper recyclables; one for garbage; and one for green waste. (Apparently, if you don't pick up your green waste instantaneously, it attracts cockroaches.) This was more like it! No more trips to the strip mall with a trunkful of ravioli cans. Perth's recycling service was even more comprehensive than Vancouver's. John and I felt much greener already.

And we were eating locally. This was entirely unconscious: most of our produce just happened to be grown in the area, because Western Australia has such a favorable growing climate. Fruit, vegetables, even wine—all fresh, plentiful, and grown in the vicinity. My mother-in-law was a big proponent of eating locally grown food.

"We can grow perfectly good oranges here," she'd say. "Why should I eat oranges grown in bloody Florida?" At the time, I just thought this was part of her anti-American stance. This was shortly after the United States invaded Iraq and Austra-lia's "arse-licker" prime minister had agreed to send troops. The Aussies weren't happy. I thought that was why my mother-in-law was boycotting American oranges, but maybe she was thinking about the carbon impact of shipping them, too?

Probably the most significant environmental change we made was becoming a one-car family again, though this had nothing to do with emissions and everything to do with the fact that a 1985 Honda Civic still cost $8,500 in Perth. And the panic attacks I suffered every time I had to drive anywhere were also a factor (valerian and Saint-John's-wort are not as calming as one might hope). Aussies drive on the wrong side of the road. While many would correct me and say the "other" side of the road, I am sticking with wrong.

Some people, like John, have little trouble switching from left to right and back again. It was not so easy for me.

"Just keep your body in the middle of the road," John advised, like it was the simplest thing in the world. It wasn't. Every time I drove, I repeated it like a mantra: "Keep your body in the middle of the road. Keep your body in the middle of the road." But a couple of right turns into oncoming traffic, and I was severely traumatized. I vowed to drive as little as possible. And now that my children were attending a school in our neighborhood, I looked forward to the brisk, twenty-minute walk each morning. It wasn't like we had to worry about the weather. Perth is invariably hot and sunny except in July and August, when it rains.

Little did I realize that Perth is invariably *hot* and sunny, with temperatures soaring up to 113 degrees Fahrenheit. It simply wasn't possible to walk briskly for twenty minutes without collapsing from heat exhaustion. I found myself driving to school on a regular basis. "Keep your body in the middle of the road. Keep your body in the middle of the road."

But we consumed a lot less in Australia. Not of food or beer or anything like that (au contraire), but I hadn't realized how much *stuff* our North American lifestyle requires: warm coats, raincoats, rain boots, snow boots, hats, gloves, scarves . . . In Australia, you don't need any of it. I had brought one jacket with me. It was new and kind of cute and I hadn't had much of a chance to wear it. I used to stare at it as it hung in the closet. "One day," I'd say, fingering the sleeve lovingly. "It can't stay hot like this forever." But apparently, it could.

While I was there, I bought a pair of Australian boots. In Canada, they cost around $180. In Australia, they were $60. What a deal!

"Do they need to be treated?" I asked the cashier as I paid for them.

He looked at me blankly.

"You know, for the weather?"

He stared. Blinked.

"Like, do I need to spray them with waterproofing spray?"

He shrugged. "I guess you could if you wanted to."

No, I didn't particularly want to. And in Perth, I didn't have to! It was a new era in low-maintenance footwear.

Another factor in our low clothing consumption was the introduction of the school uniform. All Australian public school children wear one. At first, Ethan was resistant. "I'm not wearing a uniform," he insisted. "I'll look like a dork."

"No," I assured him, "you'll look like a dork if you *don't* wear a uniform, because everyone else will be."

So we went to the Wembley Primary School store and bought two pairs of blue shorts, two blue T-shirts, one golf shirt, a sweatshirt, a pair of sweatpants, and a large, broad-brimmed hat. ("No hat: no outside play" was their motto.) That was it. For the whole year! Eventually, Ethan grew to love his uniform, and I grew to love it even more. He barely needed any other clothes! A pair of shoes, an extra pair of shorts, and a couple of T-shirts, and he was set for the year. Every country should implement public school uniforms. They're great for the planet and the pocketbook. (And that's not to mention that they're an equalizer between children of disparate incomes and that they take the emphasis off school becoming like a fashion show.)

Laundry was a different story in such a hot climate, too. Not only did we have less of it, we didn't have a dryer. At first, I was shocked. I was happy to hang clothes on the line outside, but what about when it rained? Oh right, I forgot. It never did. Since dryers account for about one-third of the energy used in a household, line-drying was great for the planet. Thanks to the blazing Australian sun, our clothes would dry in a matter of minutes. Of course, all my black clothes turned gray after about three line-dries, but it was a small price to pay.

And even in 2003, the Australians were campaigning against the plastic bag. The evil bags had been showing up in oceans and waterways and were strangling the wildlife. Endangered sea turtles were even eating these stray bags, thinking that they were jellyfish. At school, the kids painted reusable calico shopping bags. I got two very bright, very beautiful bags. And I still use them.

So despite our shaky beginnings, Australia marked a new era of environmental awareness for us. Sure, a lot of our environmental acts were sort of "accidental" (life in the Southern Hemisphere is significantly lower maintenance than it is in the colder half of the world). But Australians really cared about the future of the earth. They recycled and used reusable shopping bags. The school even had a "sibling list" so that paper newsletters were sent home with only one child per household, to save trees. And this environmental consciousness must have rubbed off on us. Even before the hard-hitting, doom-and-gloom global warming reports, we were at least starting to think about climate change. Our time in the Southern Hemisphere was the beginning of a kinder, gentler attitude toward the planet and all its creatures—except the cockroaches.   ·

Welcome to
the Green Zone

• • •

AFTER ALMOST A year of semi-green living, I told John I needed to spew another twenty tons of carbon into the atmosphere. It was time go home. My first novel was being released in North America and it was the culmination of a lifelong dream. I simply couldn't be living on the other side of the planet when it happened. I just had to convince my husband to leave his homeland and return to Canada four years early.

"It will be a lot better for my writing career if I'm back in North America," I told him. "I'll be able to do marketing and promotions and maybe even a book tour."

He didn't look convinced, so I continued.

"It's been really hard trying to coordinate phone calls with my editors in New York. I mean, when it's ten AM there, it's eleven PM here. When it's five PM there, it's six AM here—tomorrow!"

John still looked skeptical.

Fortuitously, a cockroach happened to skitter past. "Ahhhh-hhhhh! Oh god! Oh god! I can't take it anymore!"

Once again, we packed up our entire lives and moved across the planet. This time, we settled back in Vancouver. Since I had lived in Vancouver for ten years, picking a neighborhood was simple. I chose the west-side community of Kitsilano. Did it occur to me that I was choosing to relocate my family to the most expensive real estate market in Canada, where a "fixer-upper" (read: dumpy, two-bedroom shack next to a fast-food outlet) sells for well over a million dollars? No. I just wanted to live near the beach. I also didn't realize that I was moving my family to, quite possibly, the greenest neighborhood in the country.

In the sixties, "Kits" was a hotbed of hippy culture, attracting hordes of long-haired, free-loving men and women from the United States and across Canada. Greenpeace was founded in Kitsilano in 1971. And in 1983, the first offices of the Green Party of British Columbia were opened in the neighborhood. Kits has been significantly "yuppified" over the last few decades, but there are still pockets full of tree-hugging, antiestablishment types. Sure, some of these tree-hugging, antiestablishment types now have high-paying jobs, wear expensive Mountain Equipment Co-op duds, and drive pricey hybrid cars, but the hippy vibe lives on. You need only count the vegetarian restaurants, the yoga studios, and the yards with "Take Action against Climate Change" lawn signs to know that Kits residents care about the earth. They have to. It's their legacy.

We rented a bright, spacious house with nary a cockroach in sight. But the best part about our new abode was the location. Suddenly, we were so close to *everything*. We were right across the street from a large playing field, half a block from a playground and tennis courts, and two blocks from the elementary school. Jericho Beach was a ten-minute stroll away. I could walk to the grocery store, the video store, the Greek bakery, and the bank. Our neighborhood had a children's clothing store, a toy store, several shoe stores, and various adult clothing outlets. Without even trying, our carbon footprint dropped from a roomy size eight to maybe about a five.

Every morning, the kids and I walked to school (a five-minute walk, and yet somehow we still managed to rack up seventeen lates one term). And there was none of this "leaving your kid at school at lunch time means you don't love them" nonsense. We no longer had to drive across town for swimming lessons or rugby practice, either. Everything was nearby! My son joined a martial arts club literally one block away. He took guitar lessons four blocks away. In fact, my universe began to shrink to a ten-block radius. I was loath to step outside that boundary. Why would I? Everything I needed was right there.

It was 2004 now, and the state of the environment was all over the media. The world was going to end if we didn't do something—fast! And I lived in Kitsilano now. I felt a certain amount of neighborhood pressure to be kind to the planet. I hadn't quite adopted the tie-dye-and-Birkenstocks look still favored by some Kits residents, but I wanted to fit in. And I was doing a pretty good job, wasn't I? I was recycling. I turned off lights. I used green cleaning products and carried my reusable shopping bags. And I walked everywhere. Surely I was living up to the Kits environmental standard?

But then my daughter joined a dance studio several miles away. Everyone raved about this dance program. Apparently, it was the best in Western Canada and could turn Tegan into the next Karen Kain (or possibly J.Lo or Madonna). I should have been excited for her, but all I could think about was the twenty-five minute round-trip drive. My car was fairly fuel efficient, but that was still a lot of driving. It was nothing compared to someone living in L.A. or even Calgary, but in Kitsilano, it was excessive. Is this what my new neighborhood had done to me? Given me green guilt?

Still, every Tuesday, I fought my way through traffic to deliver Tegan to her dance class in the middle of Granville Island. The island, a chunk of land beneath the Granville Street Bridge, houses a huge public market and various local artisan shops and galleries. To lessen the environmental impact of the drive, I would park at the dance studio and walk to the public market to buy groceries. I only bought organic and/or local products, supporting a Vancouver industry. This went a long way to assuage my conscience. I was still being good to the environment . . . well, good-*ish*. Until they moved Tegan up a level.

"She should come three times a week," her dance instructor said.

I felt something akin to panic at the thought. First of all, she was seven! Wasn't dancing three times a week just a little *Fame*-school? Plus, how could I damage the environment by doing that drive three times every week?

I would have to cut out all extraneous driving: no more zipping downtown to meet an old friend for coffee; no more trips to the art gallery or the aquarium. Never again would I race into the city to ogle the expensive merchandise at Holt Renfrew.

Thankfully, the dance school allowed me to drop her back to two classes per week, and both were on the same night. My driving wouldn't have to increase at all. But it had gotten me thinking. While our time in Australia had kicked it off, living in Kitsilano had solidified it: I was officially trying to be kind to the environment.

"Maybe we should buy a hybrid car?" I said to John one evening.

"We will," he said, "but prices need to come down a bit."

I explained my guilt about the trips to Granville Island, which would only increase as Tegan moved up in the dance program.

"Why don't you take the bus?" John suggested.

"We barely make it there on time when we take the car! If we had to go wait at the bus stop, we'd miss the whole lesson!"

"Well, why don't you take the bus when you want to go downtown?"

"Uh . . . good idea," I said, a little embarrassed that I hadn't thought of that before. John took the bus to work every day. There were two bus stops within a block of our house. It made so much sense.

So when one of my editors was in town from Toronto and invited me to lunch on trendy Robson Street, I thought: I'll do it. I'll hop on the bus. It will be good for the environment and much simpler. It will keep me from driving around for half an hour looking for parking then forking out the kids' college tuition to pay for it.

It was cold as I headed to the bus stop. I didn't exactly have the schedule down pat, so I huddled into my stylish "lunching with the editor" coat that did little to shield me from the mid-morning chill. I waited for the bus . . . and waited. When twenty minutes had passed, I thought, surely I could have driven downtown and found a parking space in this amount of time? But no! I was being green. A real Vancouverite! Just then, a man approached me. "Good morning," he said.

"Good morning," I responded with a polite smile.

"I will pray for your soul when the giant tsunami wipes out this entire city."

"Thanks."

"God's wrath will strike down upon this city! God save your soul!"

"Great, yeah . . . my bus is here."

Good timing. I hopped on and paid my $2.25 fare. The bus driver did not give me the encouraging "thanks for giving transit a try" smile I had anticipated. He didn't even acknowledge me as he pulled the massive vehicle back onto the road. I staggered toward the back, looking for a seat. I passed two of my fellow passengers engaged in deep conversation.

"You're an asshole! You're such an asshole!"

"Look buddy, I don't even know you."

"Oh you know me all right! Asshole! Asshole!"

"I'm just trying to read my paper!"

I sat down at the back and looked out the window. Unfortunately, the window was so scratched and battered that I couldn't see a thing. I started to feel vaguely carsick—I guess bus-sick. Suddenly, the bus lurched to a stop again, letting on another handful of passengers.

A homeless man with an enormous clear plastic bag full of empty beer cans took a seat directly behind me. The aroma of stale cigarettes, rancid beer, and unwashed body overtook me. Oh god. I felt sick and dizzy and claustrophobic. I stared at the window scratches and tried to ignore the barrage of "You're an asshole! You're an asshole!" coming from a few rows up.

Finally, I reached my stop. I practically threw myself out into the relative freshness of Granville Street. I'd made it! And as I walked toward the restaurant, my nausea began to dissipate. That wasn't so bad. Okay, it was bad. It was really bad! But at least I didn't have to drive around looking for parking. No, I was actually about forty minutes early—forty minutes that I could have used to work or do laundry or something more useful. I had to stop being so negative. I took the extra time to browse in some shops before heading to my lunch date.

When I arrived at the restaurant, my editor was waiting for me. I'd never met her before, so we had much to talk about. We chatted about books in general, then my books specifically, then her job in publishing. We discussed living in Vancouver compared with living in Toronto. Finally, over coffee, I thought it was time for a humorous anecdote. She had hired me to write a humorous novel, after all. It was time to show her she hadn't wasted her money.

"So I took the bus here today," I began. "What a nightmare!" I proceeded to tell her how I wanted to be environmentally friendly, but my first transit experience in years was a disaster.

"Then this guy sat behind me with all these stinky beer cans. I almost barfed!" I continued. My editor laughed, which only served to egg me on. "My friend calls the bus the *Loser Cruiser*," I said, like I was Richard Pryor in his cocaine years. "And now I know why!"

"That's awful!" she cried. "Why don't you take a cab home?"

"I didn't bring enough money with me," I explained. "And, you know . . . I live in Kitsilano now, so I have to be green."

After lunch, my editor headed back toward her hotel. "I'll walk with you," I said, "It's on the way to my bus stop. God, my *bus stop!*" I threw up my hands for emphasis. "I can't believe I have to take the bus home. I just wish I could get into my nice, clean, warm car instead of waiting for that stinky old bus. I wish I could listen to the radio in my car instead of all the crazies swearing at each other. I hope I don't get hypothermia while I wait. It's so cold."

When we got to her hotel, my editor turned to me. "Please, take a cab," she said, shoving forty bucks into my hand. "Is this enough to get you home?"

"Oh my god!" I cried. Had she thought all my moaning was to get her to give me cab fare? I was trying to be funny, not piti-ful! On the other hand, it would be really nice to hop in the back of a warm, nice-smelling (at least comparatively) taxi. And there was a hybrid sitting right there . . .

"Twenty is enough," I said, handing back one of the bills. "It was great meeting you."

As I was chauffeured home, I felt a twinge of guilt about abandoning transit so quickly. Yes, I wanted to live up to neighborhood expectations and do my part for the environment, but I could not ride the bus again. I would walk whenever possible. I would bring my own mug to the coffee shop. I would carry my reusable shopping bags and cut my showers down to five minutes. Just don't make me ride the bus again! It was too traumatic . . . and smelly.

Leaning back into the comfortable vinyl seat of the cab, I realized that this whole green business wasn't going to be easy. I wanted to fit in with my green friends and neighbors, but there were lines I could not cross, things I would not do. I was still going to try my best to save the planet for my great-great-grandchildren, but I knew then that I'd never be the ultimate environmentalist. I just hoped I wouldn't be run out of Kitsilano.

Keeping Up
with the Greens

. . .

WE'D ONLY BEEN living in Kitsilano for a few months when my children sought out the most environmentally conscious family in the known universe and made them their best friends. I will call this family "The Greens" because they are the pinnacle of greenness, against which all other families are measured.

The Queen of Green (let's call her Valerie) is a single mother of three children. Now, if I were in her shoes, I would cut myself some slack. I'd probably feed my kids a lot of frozen pizza and send them to school with those prepackaged Lunchables. Okay, maybe I wouldn't go that far, but I would be tempted to cut a few environmental corners.

But Valerie Green is committed to doing her best for the earth, and she's not taking the easy way out. Most significantly, the Greens do not own a car. Valerie does all the grocery shopping (organic, of course) using a bike and trailer. All three kids play two musical instruments each and have a number of lessons throughout the week. Valerie shuttles the children and instruments to their lessons via bike and trailer or, in extremely inclement weather (like a blizzard), by bus. Did I mention that one of those instruments is a cello? Yes, a *cello*.

While I become exhausted just watching her, Valerie never complains. She hauls her kids to eight AM dentist appointments by bike. To birthday parties and crosstown dance classes. In the rain! At night! She broke her foot last year and still, she never asked anyone for a ride. She never took a cab!

And the Greens eat all organic food. I'm not just talking about meat and vegetables here. I'm talking organic flour, organic spices, and even organic dairy (which costs about the same as Beluga caviar). Most of their diet is locally grown, too. Valerie has personal relationships with many of the farmers in the area.

The Greens are socially conscious, as well. The children know a lot about supporting local industry and farming practices and fair-trade goods. Frankly, I don't think it's normal for children that young to be that well-informed, but maybe that's just me. My daughter had the Green girls over one day and was showing them the new shirt we'd bought for the start of the school year.

"I got this new shirt for school," Tegan said cheerfully. "It has stripes and I really like stripes."

The Green girls stared at the garment in silence. Finally, one of them said, "That shirt was made by child labor."

As my daughter's face fell, I had to intervene. "No, it wasn't," I soothed, while secretly wondering: Was it? It was awfully cheap. Was some five-year-old being paid ten cents a day to sew Tegan's cute striped shirt? But could I afford to buy clothes that were made by an adult? A wave of guilt washed over me. Why hadn't I done some research into the store's manufacturing practices? I didn't deserve to live in this neighborhood. On this planet!

While I'm making a valiant attempt to be green, I can't help but feel inadequate when I compare myself to Valerie. Last summer, John and I went to the Superstore while our kids were having a play date at the Green house. "Don't tell Valerie that we were at the Superstore," I said as we drove to retrieve our children.

"Why not?" he asked.

"Well, because . . . we drove all that way just to get a hand blender. That's bad for the environment. Plus, we bought a bunch of other stuff that we don't even need, which is really consumerist. I don't know . . . I just don't want her to know."

"Okay . . ." he said, like I'd asked him to lie and say we'd been volunteering to read stories to blind kids.

Valerie Green is far too nice to overtly judge me, but I know I'm not living up to her standards. And she is not the only one. Despite my best efforts, Kitsilano is crawling with people who are so committed to the earth that they make me feel like a property developer in comparison. We live near Broadway, a beautiful street lined with vegetable markets, Greek bakeries, and old, leafy trees. Unfortunately, because of poor sidewalk construction the sprawling roots of these old leafy trees were buckling the pavement. The Broadway sidewalks had become like some kind of treacherous urban mountain range. One day, I'd seen an elderly woman trip on a jutting piece of concrete and fall to the ground. Another time, a woman who dared to wear a bit of a heel on her shoe was felled, as well.

"Damn sidewalks," she muttered, as she scrambled to her feet. "They really need to be fixed." Eventually, when hospital emergency rooms were overflowing with victims of the Broadway sidewalks, the city got involved. They decided that the sidewalks had to be repaved. Unfortunately, they felt the easiest solution was to cut down all of the old, leafy trees.

I was walking my children home from school one chilly, rainy, miserable day when I was approached by a neighbor. "Are you coming to the rally to save the trees on Broadway?" she asked.

I huddled deeper into my raincoat, trying to ignore the biting wind whipping my face. "Uh . . . when is it?"

"Tomorrow morning at nine," she said brightly.

I could not think of anything I wanted to do less than stand around in the cold and rain chanting "Save the Trees" at nine o'clock on a Saturday morning. I did want the trees to be saved, of course I did. It would be a terrible shame if they were cut down. But was there possibly a warmer, drier way to save them?

"Do you think the weather will be like this tomorrow?" I ventured to ask.

"That's what the forecast says."

"It's just that I have a bit of a sore throat." I coughed lamely. "And I've got a lot of work to do so . . . I don't want to get sick."

She gave me a look that said: I can't believe you'd let a little rain and a sore throat keep you from saving the life of a beautiful, carbon-replenishing maple tree.

She was right. I was selfish to put my comfort above the lives of my neighborhood trees. I felt bad. I felt guilty. But I also felt cold and wet and I had a bit of a sore throat.

Thankfully, Kitsilano is full of people with bigger hearts and tougher constitutions than mine. They weren't going to let a little rain or the sniffles keep them from making a point. The city was not going to harm a leaf on those trees without getting a fight. And it worked! The Broadway trees were saved (except for six that weren't healthy and had to come down anyway).

It was on yet another rainy November day when my environmentally conscious neighbor, Melanie, left me a voice message. "Just thought I'd let you know that it's 'Buy Nothing Day,'" she said.

"Buy Nothing Day." Well, it was already two in the afternoon and I hadn't spent a dime. This wasn't going to be a problem. I would unite with my green friends and neighbors and take a stand against capitalism. I'd recently read an article by Adriana Barton in *Granville* magazine talking about the whole "green marketing" phenomenon. Some ad campaigns seemed determined to make us believe that buying up a bunch of "green" products was saving the environment. Really, the most sustainable thing to do was to buy nothing at all. And that's what I was going to do . . . today, anyway.

But when I was cooking dinner that night (wild salmon patties with, organic, olive-oil-and-rosemary frozen French fries), I realized we were out of ketchup. I can't eat organic olive-oil-and-rosemary French fries without ketchup. (Because they're so natural and healthy, they're also rather dry.) But did condiments count on "Buy Nothing Day"? Of course they didn't. "Buy Nothing Day" was probably more about people buying TVs and computer systems and Jet Skis. I sent John off to the corner store for a bottle of ketchup.

The next morning, I dropped the kids off at school and met Melanie on the playground. "Don't forget," she said. "It's 'Buy Nothing Day' today."

"Today?" I cried, "I thought it was yesterday!"

"No, it's today," she explained, "Friday, November 23."

"Well, I bought nothing yesterday," I said. (I didn't think the ketchup was worth mentioning.) "And I haven't bought anything today either," I continued, "though I need to get some wine for tonight."

Melanie looked at me. "It's 'Buy Nothing Day.'"

"But consumables don't count."

She gave a shrug that clearly said "They actually do."

Damn it! I was really looking forward to a glass of wine that night. It was Friday, after all. It was November. It had been a long week. Melanie noticed my crestfallen demeanor.

"What could you do so you don't have to buy wine?"

"If you're going to say meditate," I snapped, "don't bother."

She chuckled. "No, I'm just wondering if you had anything on hand that could relax you?"

I thought about the near-empty bottle of gin in my freezer. I could drink that, but I'd still have to buy tonic. If I was going to buy tonic, I may as well buy wine, right?

"I don't know," I sulked. "I think I have some valerian left over from my last nervous breakdown. I could take a bunch of that and just lie around on the couch drooling all night."

Again with the laughter! She wasn't taking my quandary seriously.

When John got home, he was able to allay my concerns. "Yeah, consumables don't count," he said breezily. "I'll go to the liquor store." As he was about to walk out the door, he made a suggestion. "Should we order Chinese food tonight?"

It was tempting. As I said, it had been a long week. "But it's 'Buy Nothing Day.'"

"We just decided consumables don't count."

True, but Melanie lived right around the corner. She clearly thought that consumables *did* count. What if she happened to walk by just as the delivery guy was coming up the front steps with six styrofoam containers full of ginger beef and lemon chicken? And John was returning home from the liquor store with a bottle of wine and a six-pack? What would she think of me then? She was expecting me to be lying drooling on the couch, not drinking wine and ordering takeout!

And I knew that, as North Americans, we already consume too much of everything: food, wood, energy . . . If the whole world lived like us, we'd need twenty Earths or something like that. So surely I could go without Chinese food on "Buy Nothing Day"?

"No, I'll cook."

John laughed. He was used to my guilty conscience.

"But still," I said, "go get the wine."

Yes, I sometimes feel the need to lie to my super-green

friends, but it's not because they're overtly judgmental. The Kitsilano greenies don't mean to be exclusive. In fact, they're actually a very welcoming bunch. One Sunday, Tegan and I walked to the local farmers' market, our reusable shopping bags swinging jauntily from our hands. As we entered the bustling scene, I was approached by a pleasant, middle-aged woman who handed me a flier.

"Come join us at the Global Warming Café," she invited, smiling warmly.

I looked at the piece of paper. The café was a place where people from the neighborhood could get together to share ideas and strategies to protect the environment. What a great concept! And it was being held at the community center only a few blocks from my house. I would attend next Sunday.

I kept the Global Warming Café flier on my desk all week and marked the date on my calendar. This was going to be great. I was really becoming a part of the green community. And I was really going to make a contribution to the planet. The URL was featured prominently on the flyer, so I decided to check out their Web site beforehand.

"Click here to see photos of previous Global Warming Cafés," the site invited me. So I clicked. As I stared at the photos, I suddenly realized I couldn't go. Everyone looked so knowledgeable and passionate and deep, dark, forest green. They were all wearing clothes from Mountain Equipment Co-op. There were several women there with long gray hair in braids. I didn't belong. I wouldn't fit in. I wasn't green enough.

They would take one look at me and they would know. I had highlights! Obviously, someone who would choose to put harsh chemicals into her hair and, subsequently, down the drain, didn't really care about the planet. Someone too vain and superficial to let her hair go gray naturally would have nothing to contribute regarding the environment. And what would I wear? I owned no MEC threads, no hemp or soy or thrift-shop finds. Yes, I had a vegan purse, but how far would that get me? My coat was probably made by a nine-year-old in Bangladesh. No, as soon as I walked through the door they'd recognize my type: the type who *says* she cares about the environment, but owns too many pairs of shoes and won't take the bus and drives all the way to the Superstore just to get a hand blender!

I love living in Kitsilano. And I'm really thankful for the residents who put up signs, hand out fliers, and organize mailings and protest rallies. Every time I walk along Broadway, admiring the way the leaves dapple the sidewalk with their shadows and rustle gently in the breeze, I am grateful to my neighborhood rabble-rousers. But, much like riding the bus, I just can't bring myself to their level of activism. This realization makes me worry a bit. Do I really fit in here? Or am I just too selfish and lazy to live up to my neighborhood's green standards?

An Oasis of Green

EVEN AFTER LIVING in Kits for a few years, I was still falling way short of the Kitsilano green ideal. I wasn't marching with my neighbors to save trees and heritage buildings. I hadn't been on the bus since that last nerve-wracking ride downtown. And I was still buying impossibly cheap clothing for my kids. The guilt was starting to get to me. I had to do something.

"Let's green the house!" I suggested to John.

"Sure," he said. "There are lots of things we can do to make it more energy efficient." John works at BC Hydro so he's kind of "up" on that kind of stuff.

First, he went to the hardware store and bought a water-saving kit. It included a low-flow showerhead (we'd buy another one for the second shower later); water aerators to limit the water flow from our faucets; and a toilet tank bank (basically a plastic bag that you fill, snap closed, and hang in your toilet tank so the toilet uses less water for flushing). He set right to work installing them. By that evening, we were a much greener household.

After dinner, I went to hook up the dishwasher. (Ours is an older house, so we still have to manually attach the dishwasher hose to the kitchen faucet.)

"It doesn't fit," I said, trying to press the nozzle onto the spout.

"It's the water aerator," John explained. "We'll have to take it off every time we use the dishwasher."

"Seriously?" I asked. I had just gotten used to not having a built-in dishwasher. Now I had to wrench a fixture off every time I hooked up the water hose? "Why don't we just take this aerator off?" I suggested. "We've still got them on all the other faucets. We're still being good."

That night, I sent the kids for their showers. Since our water-conservation kit came with only one showerhead, we had put it on the upstairs shower. I sent the kids up there. "Try the new showerhead," I said. "It's better for the environment."

Ethan showered without comment. But when Tegan was finished, she announced that the new showerhead was "terrible."

"I hate that shower," she said. "There's not enough water. I was freezing the whole time. I'm never having a shower upstairs again."

I went to John and spoke in a hushed voice. "She hates the low-flow showerhead. Maybe we shouldn't bother getting one for downstairs?"

"But if we have low-flow showerheads in both bathrooms, she'll have no choice. Don't worry, she'll get used to it."

He obviously had a higher tolerance for whining than I did. "But she'll moan and groan every time she has to take a shower. And when she gets out, we'll have to listen to her whine about how cold she is. Let's just have one low-flow showerhead. It's more than a lot of people have. We're still good."

Later that night, I prepared for bed. I brushed my teeth then turned my energy-efficient faucet to warm so I could wash my face. I let the trickle of water run for a few seconds then tested the temperature: freezing. I waited and tried again: still freezing. It took almost eight minutes for the temperature to change to lukewarm.

"It's the water aerator," John said. "Less water is flowing so it takes longer for the cold water to flush through the pipes and the warm water to come in."

I was tempted to ask him to remove it right then and there. It was late and I was exhausted. I didn't want to stand around for ten minutes waiting for warm water. What was this, the eighteen hundreds? But I'd already removed one water aerator and aborted plans for a second low-flow showerhead. My home was falling far short of the green oasis I'd intended. I could live with the cool water. At least I thought I could.

I lasted several weeks—or maybe it just felt like several weeks and was only a couple of days. Either way, the water aerator had to go. Letting the water run for ten minutes wasn't good for the environment! And washing my face in ice water was not an option. I have enough trouble falling asleep, even without an invigorating, bedtime splash of cold water in the face. John removed the aerator for me.

Once again, I was feeling a little inadequate in the green department. Despite our good, water-saving intentions, we were practically back to square one. Sure, our toilets were using less water, but we now had only one low-flow showerhead and one low-flow faucet. We weren't good—we were merely sufficient.

Then John came home from work with a whole bunch of compact fluorescent lightbulbs. "They were handing them out free at work," he explained. "The marketing department did some big promotion with them awhile ago, and they had a bunch left over."

"Great!" I said, back on the green-home bandwagon. "Free bulbs!" I knew that compact fluorescent lightbulbs (CFLs) cost more than regular lightbulbs, but they used much less energy and lasted a lot longer. I would have been happy to shell out the money, but this was even better. We changed all our incandescent bulbs to CFLs. The new lighting was a little hard to get used to at first. The bulb in our reading lamp seemed to be a little on the dim side, while the overhead lights in the kitchen were exceedingly bright. And the ones above the bathroom vanity were positively blinding! (At a certain age, it's not good to see your face in that much detail.) But eventually, we grew accustomed to them.

Obviously our new lightbulbs were a step in the right direction. But I was watching the news one night when a report came on about CFLs. "We all know that compact fluorescent lightbulbs use less energy," the anchorman said gravely, "but you may not know that they also contain DEADLY MERCURY!" (Okay, maybe he didn't say those exact words, but that was the gist.)

I called to John in the kitchen. "Come quick! Our new lightbulbs contain deadly mercury!"

"Yeah, I know," he said, strolling in casually.

"You know?" I screeched. "So what does that mean? Are our new lightbulbs poisoning us with mercury vapor? Is our hair going to fall out? Will we all get brain cancer?"

"No," he said calmly, "it just means we have to recycle them properly."

I turned my attention back to the news. After such a terror-inducing lead-in, that's basically what the report was saying. CFLs were still better for the environment than incandescent bulbs. They just had to be recycled properly when they burned out. Phew!

So for a while, we were feeling quite smug in our greenness. "We're pretty damn green," John said one night, as we huddled under a blanket, straining our eyes to read by the dim light of our compact fluorescent lightbulb.

"We are," I agreed. "We're really doing our part."

And then a new Costco opened up in nearby Yaletown. My neighbor told me about it. "A huge jar of organic peanut butter is only five bucks," she said.

That alone was worth the price of membership. We ate a lot of peanut butter. Valerie Green had told me that peanuts soak up pesticides and also create some kind of weird mold (her kids ate only almond butter). But we loved peanut butter. And organic peanut butter must be okay, right? But at the natural food store, even a small jar was five dollars. We had to become Costco members.

My green guilt was tingling a little as we drove down to the massive warehouse. An enormous wholesale store didn't feel very environmentally friendly. We were supposed to be consuming less, weren't we? But buying in bulk did cut down on packaging. It made sense to buy one enormous jar of peanut butter instead of five smaller ones. I just had to control my buying behavior.

But as soon as I walked through those gaping doors, something happened to me. I turned into the megaconsumer. I didn't care about being green and buying less. Everything was so cheap! I ran down the aisles like a hyperactive kid in a candy store.

"I don't really need nine deodorant sticks, but it's such a good deal!"

"If I buy a case of mustard now, I won't need to buy more until 2011!"

"A box of four hundred tampons should get me through to menopause!"

The shopping list I'd painstakingly made sat neglected in my pocket. I wasn't going to limit myself. I *needed* that gallon jar of artichoke hearts. And a three-pack of lounge pants! How had I lived so long without a pair of lounge pants? Obviously I needed three of them. When we got to the till, our bill came to over three hundred dollars.

The temporary high of accumulation soon gave way to megaconsumer's remorse. There I was, trying to green my home, and I'd just spent three hundred dollars on toothpaste and mustard and lounge pants that I didn't really need. I had to do something to make up for my overconsumption.

"Let's only use recycled paper products from now on," I said to my husband. I had been reading Laurie David's book *Stop Global Warming: The Solution Is You!* It said that if every household in America replaced just one roll of regular toilet paper with recycled toilet paper, they would save 424,000 trees.

"Sure," he agreed.

The next time I went shopping, I bought an eight-pack of recycled toilet paper. Maybe I was only saving half a tree with this purchase, but over the course of our family's butt-wiping lifetime, it was sure to add up. I felt really good about it, until I got a rash.

Yes, I'm embarrassed to admit this, but I feel consumers should be warned. Recycled toilet paper gave me a rash. And what a bad place to get a rash! I had to stop using the stuff right then and there. Maybe I have an extra-sensitive bottom, but I was in agony. I wanted to save trees, I really did. But I wasn't going to walk around scratching my ass every five minutes.

"Okay, so from now on we'll use super-soft toilet paper, but recycled paper towels and tissues," I explained to John.

"Got it," he said. But he hadn't got it. He went grocery shopping and came home with two eight-packs of regular tissues.

"This isn't recycled," I said, looking at the eight boxes wrapped in plastic.

"It was on sale."

I looked closer. "This has lotion on it. That's even worse!"

"Why?" John asked.

"Uh..." I didn't know why but, in my annoyance, I felt compelled to make up a reason. "It's not real lotion. They use lotion *chemicals*. Those lotiony chemicals will soak into the soil when all this tissue ends up in a landfill."

"Okay," John said, "I'll remember to get recycled next time."

"Next time? We've got sixteen boxes of this stuff! Next time could be in a year!"

I knew John wanted to be green as much as I did. But for some reason, he didn't seem to suffer from the same sickening sense of guilt. Why was that? What was wrong with me?

A few days later, I was chatting with my friend Trevor, who is very green. He and his partner were renovating their house using as many environmentally friendly measures as possible. They'd installed low-emission, argon-filled, double-pane windows to keep UV rays out and heat in. An on-demand tankless water heater was much more energy-efficient than their old one. They'd ripped up and then re-laid their old floorboards after installing in-floor heating. And they'd torn out their inefficient fireplace and replaced it with an ultra-efficient woodstove. Unfortunately, renovating "green" was significantly more expensive than just plain renovating, and they'd soon exceeded their budget.

"It sucks that everything good for the environment is so damned expensive," I commiserated.

"I know," he agreed. "And apparently, if everyone in the world just unplugged all their appliances at night, we could basically stop global warming."

"What?!"

"Yeah," he explained, "Even when household appliances are off, they continue to draw energy. They're called energy vampires."

My publisher had given me an advance copy of a British book called *The Hot Topic* (written by Gabrielle Walker and Sir David King). Imagine my surprise when the authors mentioned the very same subject. The book said that devices left in "standby mode" cost the world a full one percent of our greenhouse gas emissions—nearly as much as the entire aviation industry!

Then, about a week later, Oprah did a show on easy ways to be green. Her environmental expert suggested we plug all appliances into a power bar and turn it off every night. I didn't need to be told three times. We were going to do it!

"John!" I cried. "We have to start unplugging everything!"

So John went into the basement storage room and found an old power bar. He connected our TV, VCR, DVD player, and stereo to this power strip, and we switched it off every night. I was also good about unplugging the toaster, coffeemaker, and my cell-phone charger. (I started leaving the microwave plugged in when I got tired of resetting the clock every morning.)

Now I just had to get everyone else in the world to do this, and we could stop worrying about all this eco-crap. We could fly guilt-free again. Take long, hot showers. Drive big cars! In Australia, all power outlets have an on-and-off switch. Why the hell don't we have that here?

I decided to mention my brilliant plan to stop global warming to a group of moms on the school playground one day.

"Nothing can stop global warming now," one of them said. "Sure, we can slow it down, but no matter what we do as the human race..."

"Stop!" I wanted to scream at her. "I just put in trickling showerheads and dim lightbulbs. I got an ass-crack rash from recycled toilet paper and you're telling me there's no hope? Don't be so depressing!" But what would that do to my reputation in the neighborhood? Instead, I just pasted on a smile and nodded along.

The Environmental
Zealot

• • •

EVEN WITH MY low-flow showerhead and compact fluorescent lightbulbs, I knew that I wasn't as green as I could be. There was so much more I could do. I could be collecting rainwater run off for washing my dishes. I could have installed a clothesline for drying the laundry. And I still didn't have a bucket of vegetable waste–eating worms living under my sink. But was I really willing to go that extra mile? I still cared an awful lot about comfort and convenience. Maybe I was just too selfish to be truly green?

"You're *very* environmentally friendly," my mom assured me, squirting some of my phosphate-free dish soap into the trickle of water coming from my faucet. "I think it's great."

"I'm not *that* great," I said modestly, "I'm just trying my best to save the planet for future generations."

Since my mom was so supportive of my green streak, I thought maybe she'd appreciate me sharing my wisdom about the environment. Because I knew she cared about the planet—she recycled and carried reusable shopping bags. But a woman her age was understandably not quite as "in the know" as someone like me, who had her finger on the pulse. Besides, her generation had a decidedly different view of what it meant to care about the earth. To them, using recycled toilet paper was tantamount to chaining yourself to a tree in a logging protest. I decided I would educate her. I was going to *green* my mom.

We were having a family dinner at her house one evening. "Please don't microwave that plastic wrap," I said as I watched her put a bowl of broccoli covered in plastic wrap into the microwave.

"Why? Is that going to kill me now too?"

"Yes. The plastic leaches into your food when it's heated and causes cancer. And plastic wrap never biodegrades. And by the way, microwaves change the molecular structure of your food or something like that."

"I've never trusted microwaves," she said.

"I remember. I think we were the last family in Quesnel to get one."

"Looks like I was right." Agreeably, my mom removed the plastic wrap. "I'll put this broccoli into something with a lid."

That went well. My mom really appreciated my life- and Earth-saving tip. Even if I couldn't be super-green myself, by spreading the green word, I was really helping the planet!

A few weeks later, my mom was at my house for a visit. She

was commenting on how much water I drank. (About twelve glasses a day. I go pee about twenty-seven times.) "I'm really trying to drink more water," she said. "I find that if I keep bottles of water in the fridge, I drink a lot more."

"You can't do that," I responded. "It's bad for the environment."

"Well, I recycle them," she said, a little defensively.

"Oh mom." I chuckled ruefully. "Yes, recycling your bottles is better than throwing them in the garbage, but it still uses a lot of energy and water. It's much better to just drink tap water in a glass. Do you think you can make that change?"

My mom looked a little less appreciative of my environmental suggestion this time. In fact, she looked just a tad irritated by my enlightening advice.

But as her eldest child, wasn't it my duty to make sure she was saving the earth for future generations? Since I was doing a half-assed job myself, shouldn't I ensure that my mother was making an effort as well?

"I'm driving to Kelowna to get sixty pounds of peaches for canning," she told me. "My friend has an orchard there."

"You're *driving* almost 200 miles to Kelowna for peaches?" I asked. "I hope you're not taking your enormous truck."

"Well, yes," she retorted, "I'm buying sixty pounds of peaches. I have to have somewhere to put them."

I shook my head. "That's a lot of emissions just so you can enjoy canned peaches on your cereal. And by the way, are they organic?"

And another time . . .

"I'm repainting the townhouse."

"Have you bought the paint yet?" I asked. "Because, according to *Ecoholic*, you should really be buying low-VOC paints. Regular paint has all sorts of toxic chemicals that pollute the air and cause health problems."

"I've already bought it," she snapped. "I've lived with toxic paint all my life and it hasn't hurt me so far."

And also. . .

"Would you like to come for Easter dinner?" my mom asked. "I'll cook a turkey."

"Sure," I replied. "Will you be sure to get a turkey that was raised cage-free and make sure it's unmedicated?"

My mom just looked at me. And this time, her look went beyond annoyance. This time, her look clearly said: "Oh Christ. Why did my only daughter grow up to be such an annoying environmental zealot?"

Was she right? Was I becoming an annoying environmental zealot? How could I be? I'd removed my water aerators and refused to take public transit. I didn't preach and proselytize about the depressing state of the planet. I didn't tsk and sneer when I saw someone committing a less-than-green act. Okay, maybe I did tsk and sneer when I saw someone driving a Hummer, but that was as much about the pretention as the emissions. No, I wasn't an environmental zealot. I was just. . . helpful.

The next morning, the kids and I were walking to school. As we passed by a neighbor's house, I noticed his car idling in the driveway. "See that, kids," I said, pointing out the running car.

"That's very bad for the environment. And Vancouver has a no-idling law."

Now, if I were an environmental zealot, I would have knocked on that guy's door and read him the riot act. I would have spouted off statistics about how idling for more than ten seconds uses more fuel than restarting your car (according to the City of Vancouver's Web site onedayvancouver.ca). I would have handed him a pamphlet about the end of the world. I would have yanked his keys out of the ignition and chucked them into his hydrangea bush. Did I do any of that? No. I just shot him some "eye daggers" when he came out of his house, and left it at that.

When we arrived at school, we walked past a number of minivans pulling up to the curb to drop off their charges. (Yes, even in Kitsilano there are rebels.) I knew that at least two of those families lived only three or four blocks away. If I were, in fact, an over-the-top environmentalist, I would have tapped on the window. "Why don't you try getting up a few minutes earlier so you can walk to school?" I would have said. "Amanda and her kids live farther away than you do, and they do it every day." But I remained mute. I didn't want a reputation as the irritating green guilt-tripper. And I wasn't an environmental zealot, no matter what my mom thought.

But it appeared this was a familial opinion. My brother Scott seemed to agree with our mother. It all started with a forwarded e-mail. I hate getting forwarded e-mails as much as the next person. I hate when I get the same stupid joke from six different people, or worse—the "forward this on or you will be murdered by the ghost of Jeffrey Dahmer in your sleep"–type of chain letter. But this was an important issue.

One of my greenie friends had sent me an environmental petition to sign. It was during the December 2007 UN summit on climate change in Bali. Canada had been given the "fossil award" for being the worst country in the world on climate change. The worst country in the *world!* How could we just stand by and let our reputation be damaged like that? If we all signed the petition it would show our government that the Canadian people really did care about the environment. We were the good guys.

So I signed it. It took all of ten seconds to click and add my name to the petition. When I'd done it, I thought: I'm going to do the right thing. I'm going to forward this on so other people can take the simple yet Earth-saving step and sign it too. And my brother Scott just happened to be on my e-mail list.

A few days later, I got a phone call from Scott. "I got that e-mail thing you sent the other day," he said coolly. "Yeah . . . thanks for that." Like I'd sent him a membership form for my pyramid scheme . . . or a box full of steaming dog crap! It was just a click and type. It took ten seconds!

"Well, it actually worked," I retorted. "I got an e-mail today saying that a climate change agreement was finally reached."

"Great," he said, with as much enthusiasm as someone about to have a wart burnt off.

I was upset by his reaction, so I ratted him out to his wife.

"Scott acted like I sent him a bag of poo," I whined to my sister-in-law Kerry. "It was just an e-mail petition! I'm not annoying, am I? I mean, I'm not even that green."

"Oh, no," she said. "You're not that bad. I know people who are way worse than you are."

Didn't she really mean: "You're not that *good*. I know people who are way better."?

Scott's reaction had shaken my confidence. I knew I wasn't an out-of-control greenie, but my family was making me doubt myself. Even my green-ish brother Joel had made an enviro-crack at me. It was after a family dinner when he was washing the dishes with the water running. I just happened to helpfully mention that it was a terrible waste of water, and he said, "Go save a village, Robyn."

While the Kitsilano tree-huggers made me feel like I wasn't doing enough, my family was making me feel like the environmental equivalent of a Jehovah's Witness: obsessed with spreading the word about the end of the world. I was confused and conflicted. I was torn between two worlds. That's when I knew I was going "enviro-mental"—I was being driven crazy by guilt, confusion, and worry about the environment.

Can We Afford to Eat Organic? Can We Afford Not To?

• • •

WASN'T GOING TO lose my mind. I had children to think about, and a sane mother was obviously better than one who was locked up in the psych ward. No longer would I attempt to live up to other people's environmental expectations—or live down to them, as the case may be. I was going to focus on my family, and to hell with the outside world (well, not to *hell with it,* as my green choices were bound to have some sort of impact on the planet overall). I decided to focus on our diet.

By this time, I was aware that organic food wasn't just good for our health; it was good for the earth, too. In Calgary and Australia, organic produce hadn't been so readily available. But in Vancouver, there were a couple of stores in the area devoted to the stuff. Even our regular grocery store had a large organic section. Sure, it cost a little more, but maybe it was worth it. Ethan forced me to examine the issue.

"So . . . why is some food organic and some food not?" He asked as we walked to school one morning.

"Well," I explained, "some people prefer to eat food that hasn't been sprayed with pesticides and some people don't really care."

Ethan was shocked. "So some people actually say: I'd rather have that apple that's been sprayed with DDT and pesticides that will give me cancer?"

"Well, organic food is a lot more expensive."

Tegan asked, "But shouldn't organic food be cheaper, you know, since they don't have to pay for all that poison?"

"Unfortunately, that's not how it works." I took a deep breath and attempted to explain supply and demand. "When apples are sprayed with pesticides, the bugs don't eat them. That means farmers can grow more apples and they can sell them for less money."

So," I turned to Ethan, "what if that organic apple was three dollars and the apple that was sprayed with poison was only fifty cents? Which one would you eat then?"

He gaped at me. "Not the poison one!"

He had a point. And while the link between pesticides and cancer is still being studied, logic dictates that eating bug killer can't be good for you. So I decided to suck it up and buy that three-dollar apple. And that four-dollar thumb of ginger. For a month, I was strictly organic—and then I looked at my bank statement.

I imagined all the things I could have bought with the money I'd spent on organic food! Like shoes . . . for the entire family. New tires for the car. Laser eye surgery! The difference was substantial: $2.98 for a head of organic cauliflower, or $1.78 for a conventional one. A head of organic lettuce was $3.00. Regular, poisonous lettuce was only $1.28. Organic zucchini: $2.98 a pound. Conventional zucchini: $1.28 a pound. Organic ginger: $9.98 a pound. Conventional ginger: $5.98 a pound.

And it's not like the organic label was clear-cut and straightforward. A friend had told me that you had to buy *certified* organic food, otherwise there were no guarantees that the farmer had followed organic practices at all. So I was scouring labels looking for the critical *"certified"* when another friend told me it didn't really matter. He said that there were plenty of farmers growing "organic" produce who weren't certified, and that certification was expensive and designed to suit huge, industrialized farms and not the small, responsible farmer. Great! Ambiguous, confusing, *and* expensive! This eating organic stint just kept getting better and better.

The conventional produce taunted me. There it sat at the sidewalk markets, all fresh and cheap and locally grown. But no . . . my family could not ingest those horrible chemicals! Or could they?

I mean, how bad could they really be for you? Sure they could kill a bug, but even Tegan was like, five hundred times the size of a bug. Besides, we were probably immune after our year in Australia living in Casa Bug Spray. So maybe it wouldn't hurt to eat some conventional produce? Perhaps only when the organic alternative was too pricey? Or would I rue that decision when we all got some horrific pesticide-related tumor on our salivary glands?

And then, a friend of mine gave me a copy of a magazine. "I thought you might be interested in this," she said.

I looked at the cover of the *Chatelaine* she proffered. "Is organic food worth the $$$?" the headline read. Finally! I would have the answer I'd been seeking. I thanked my friend profusely and hurriedly flipped to the article. Eagerly, I perused the introductory paragraph. Writer Diane Peters had studied the research, talked to health experts, and eaten a ton of organic foods and their conventional counterparts. From all her work, she was able to answer my nagging question with a resounding "Sometimes."

Though the article was a little dated, it was better than nothing. This article became somewhat of a shopping guide for me. For example, it said that consumers should shell out the extra money for organic apples, bell peppers, grapes, pears, raspberries, and strawberries (I basically took this to mean all fruit without a really thick peel) because these foods showed high levels of pesticide residue. It also recommended eating organic lettuce and spinach, as well as root vegetables such as beets and potatoes. In contrast, it said that conventional asparagus, avocados, bananas, broccoli, cauliflower, corn, onions, and peas typically carry fewer pesticides.

It wasn't quite as specific a guide as I'd been looking for, but it would have to do. I decided I would make an effort to buy the organic produce the article recommended, when it wasn't too expensive. When it was? Well, eating a few pesticides probably wasn't going to kill us. In fact, it would probably allow our

bodies to build up resistance to fight the poisons we were ingesting. I thought this was a pretty good solution. My son thought
differently.

I'm not sure where his pious attitude toward conventional
fruits and vegetables developed. School? Playground chitchat?
Some hard-hitting documentary he'd seen about pesticides
causing tumors in rats?

Perhaps I could blame the vegan chef who lived in the basement suite? But he was such a nice guy. He'd planted a garden
in the backyard and given the kids a few plants for themselves.
We'd lovingly planted them and watched the beans, cucumbers, squash, and tomatoes grow. But since we were organic
farmers, everything was ravaged by insects, and our crop yield
was precisely two beans (which I, nevertheless, steamed and
fed to the kids).

I didn't really think my downstairs neighbor had been
secretly inundating my children with vegan philosophy. But
something had turned Ethan into an organic fanatic. Every
morsel of food he put in his mouth was accompanied by the
question, "Is this organic?" When the answer was "yes," there
was no problem. But when I had to answer "no," I felt the need
to justify my purchase.

"But it's local, at least."

"It's hot-house grown so it's *virtually* pesticide free."

"The organic grapes were like, nine dollars a bunch!"

Ethan would grudgingly finish his snack, but with an
expression on his face that said, "When I have children, I won't
be too cheap to ensure they're eating the healthiest option and
protecting the planet for future generations."

It got worse. He then went through a phase where he would pretend to projectile vomit every time he ate conventional food. "Is this organic?" he'd ask.

"No," I'd ruefully reply.

"Bwaaaaaaaaaaaaa!" He'd pretend to spew his cereal all over the table and then chuckle heartily at his own joke. It was so much fun that it became constant.

"Is this juice organic?"

"No," I snapped. "Organic juice is too expensive. Not everything you put in your mouth has to be organic, you know."

"Bwaaaaaaaaaaaaa!" he'd say, then laugh his head off.

Luckily, the fake barfing eventually grew tiresome, but his pious attitude remained. This was nothing more than a minor irritant until he took it outside the home.

The kids had gone to stay with my mom for a few days. When she brought them back, she said something like: "Wow, Ethan's really picked up your environmental zealotry." (That's probably not exactly what she said, but that's how I heard it.)

"Oh god. What did he say?"

"We had asparagus with dinner. Ethan asked if it was organic, and I said no. He refused to eat it."

"That's because he hates asparagus," I explained, "not because he's an environmental zealot."

"Well," my mom continued, "Tegan was eating hers and he pointed and laughed at her: "Ha ha, you're eating pesticides.""

I decided to talk to him. "Can you give the whole organic thing a bit of a rest?"

"Why?" he asked.

"Well . . . people find it kind of annoying when you constantly ask if things are organic. Some people just don't care about eating organic."

"Why?" he asked.

"I don't know. They just don't, okay? Can you please just drop it?"

Apparently, he didn't hear me. About a week later, we were at my nephew's birthday party. "Auntie Kerry?" Ethan asked as he eyed the fruit-and-veggie platter. "Are these strawberries organic?"

"No, they're not."

"These carrots? This cantaloupe? These peppers?"

"Nothing's organic, Ethan," she said, a trace of annoyance in her voice. "You need to chill out on the organic thing."

I saw a couple I didn't recognize looking at Ethan with bewilderment. What's wrong with that kid, they were wondering. Is he on some special pesticide-free diet? Does he live on some sort of commune? Is he David Suzuki's long-lost love child?

"We live in Kitsilano," I said, by way of explanation.

"Ohhhhh." They nodded knowingly.

When it was time for cake, Ethan lined up with the other kids. "Oh, sorry," Auntie Kerry said, "This cake's not organic, Ethan. Are you sure you want some?"

Of course, conventional birthday cake and conventional asparagus are two different things. Ethan threw caution to the wind and had a huge piece.

Ethan had just mellowed on the organic thing when the "eat local" wave hit. Organic suddenly didn't seem to matter so much. If you cared about the earth, you were supposed to be eating foods grown close to home. I'd heard about the book *The 100-Mile Diet: A Year of Local Eating* by Alisa Smith and J.B. MacKinnon. The Vancouver couple had subsisted on foods cultivated and harvested within one hundred miles of their home. I considered reading it. I even vaguely considered following their diet, but I have a psychological issue with the word diet (whenever I feel restricted I just want to gorge myself on Dairy Queen Blizzards). While I wouldn't go whole-hog, I decided to become more conscious of where my food came from. We were going to become "locavores."

I was already doing quite well. BC Hot House provided affordable, locally grown bell peppers, cucumbers, and tomatoes, and I was a big fan. Their Web site (www.bchothouse.com) also stated that greenhouse-grown vegetables were "virtually pesticide free." (They release a bunch of wasps and ladybugs into the greenhouse, which eat all the nasty, plant-eating bugs.) The produce was also grown hydroponically in natural, biodegradable materials like rock wool and woodchips. Obviously, this was an excellent choice.

So I was feeling very noble as I stood in my vegetable market, filling my grocery basket with BC Hot House–grown produce. Then an elderly couple approached me.

"You know that BC Hot House tomatoes are actually grown in Mexico," the man said.

"Is that right?" I replied patronizingly. The poor guy was obviously senile.

"You've got to be careful," his wife added. "You can't trust companies to label things properly. They can be misleading."

"Mmm hmm," I said dismissively, going about my shopping. Those paranoid old people weren't going to make me second-guess myself. Obviously this tomato with the BC Hot House sticker on it wasn't grown in Mexico. It was grown in BC!

A few months later I saw an article in the spring 2008 issue of *Granville* magazine. "Seeking Certification" was all about how food labelled "local" or "organic" isn't necessarily the best environmental choice. "That's just freaking great," I muttered as I started to read. I could feel the uncomfortable (and now familiar) stirrings of enviro-mentalism. The words jumped right out at me in bold print. BC Hot House tomatoes were grown in Mexican greenhouses in the winter. The paranoid old people were right! The article went on to say that greenhouses require a lot of energy for heating and lighting, so foods grown in them are not a good environmental choice at all. Shit!

The book *The Hot Topic* concurred on the greenhouse matter. It also pointed out that, instead of just eating local, we should be calculating "food miles." It doesn't just matter how far the food has travelled; it matters *how* it's travelled. Planes contribute the most emissions, followed by trucks (though they can be fairly efficient if they are fully loaded), and then trains. So in my case, eating a peach grown in the relatively nearby Okanagan Valley and trucked to Vancouver could actually be worse for the environment than a Californian peach sent to Vancouver by train.

The book also brought up the fact that some of the poorest countries in the world grow fruit, vegetables, and flowers for some of the richest. It mentioned that exporting produce to the UK was a vital part of sub-Saharan Africa's economy, supporting up to a million and a half livelihoods. So if I decided not to buy Mexican-grown BC Hot House tomatoes, was I stealing jobs from impoverished Mexican workers? If I chose fruit from Kelowna over fruit from Ecuador, was I bankrupting an Ecuadorian farmer while the farmer in Kelowna put in a pool? That just wasn't right.

A February 2008 *New Yorker* article by Michael Specter entitled "Big Foot" elaborated on the local food issue—and made it even more convoluted. There were other factors at play in calculating a food's carbon contribution: how much lighting was needed, where the water came from, whether the growing area has a renewable energy source, what type of packaging was used, how the label was printed . . . An apple from New Zealand, the article said, could actually be more energy efficient than one grown nearby, given the prime growing conditions and use of renewable energy Down Under. (*The Hot Topic* mentioned that African produce being flown to the UK contributes less than 0.1 percent of the UK's overall greenhouse gas emissions.)

So what the hell did it all mean? Was I supposed to buy New Zealand apples now? Or only fruit that came from far away countries that were really poor? How was I supposed to know if the grower used artificial lights or irrigation or wind energy? What was I supposed to do?

The *New Yorker* article said that the European grocery giant Tesco had plans to give foods a carbon label that would inform consumers about a product's environmental impact over the course of its life cycle. The company would also label all foods shipped by air with a little airplane symbol. *The Hot Topic* said we should all be pushing our governments for this kind of food labelling, too.

It would make things much simpler... I think. As consumers, we'd be able to check carbon just like we check calories and artificial colors. But might we start to confuse the issues? "These cheese puffs are high in saturated fat and sodium but low in food miles. Let's eat them!" Or "These bananas are nutritious, delicious, and the livelihood of ten thousand Ecuadorian workers. But... they have an airplane sticker on them, so we can't buy them."

Eating green was much harder than I'd anticipated. In fact, it was tempting to just throw up my hands and go back to eating whatever I wanted. But I still cared about my family's health. And despite the confusion, I still wanted to make Earth-friendly choices. So I would try my best to be a responsible consumer. Little did I know that the confusion was only going to get worse.

Mom, Will This Chicken Give Me Man Boobs?

IT WAS A stupid choice for dinner conversation. But sometimes, a topic just springs to mind and it's out of your mouth before you can censor yourself.

"I heard that boys in America are getting breasts from the growth hormones in chicken," I casually mentioned to my husband over a meal of chicken fajitas.

"What?!" Ethan spat out the fajita he'd been chewing. His face was a mask of terror.

Oops. "Don't worry," I assured him. "It's probably not true."

"So I won't get man boobs from eating chicken?"

"No. And even if it is true, you'd probably have to eat hundreds of chicken breasts to get man boobs."

He was not appeased. "Can I have some cereal?"

"You'll be fine," I insisted. "Just eat your dinner. I'm sorry I brought it up."

John was slow to catch on. "I read online somewhere that girls in kindergarten are getting their periods from chicken hormones."

"What's a period?" Tegan, who was in kindergarten at the time, asked.

"We'll talk about it later," I said. My son already looked like he was about to faint from the prospect of getting man boobs. I didn't think it was the right time to explain menstruation.

Although I had been quick to dismiss Ethan's concerns, I was, frankly, grossed out. I had to at least look into it. The last thing I needed was to go bra shopping with my son. However, if my daughter took after me in the breast department, she could use a little boost from the hormones. But would our government really allow our meat to be treated with growth hormones that would see our boys wearing a C cup? Our girls having PMS in preschool? Perhaps I was too naïve, too trusting, but I simply couldn't believe it.

Like most North American children of the seventies, I grew up on a meat-based diet. When I'd ask my mom what was for dinner, the response was invariably: beef, chicken, or pork. The veggies and carbs (usually an iceberg salad with Thousand Island dressing and white rice or potatoes) were basically irrelevant. Wasn't I living proof that there were no hormones in Canadian meat? Or that if there were, they did nothing to enhance one's bustline?

Once again, I turned to books, magazines, and the Internet to clear up the mystery. According to *Ecoholic* and my *Chatelaine* article on organic food, Canadian chickens, lambs, and pigs are not given growth hormones, but cattle are. So if any-thing is going to cause man boobs, it's beef! Good to know. All types of animals are given various vaccines and antibiotics to keep them from getting sick in their crowded, miserable pens before their sad, miserable lives are snuffed out. (The use of these products is highest in the hog industry.)

When I first moved out of my parents' house, I didn't eat meat for many years. It wasn't a health issue for me, it was a kill-ing issue. (I also wore peace-sign earrings and went through a prolonged Doors phase.) Perhaps I can attribute my anti-meat stance to my upbringing? I was raised in the interior of BC, where ranching is a significant industry. One might think this would toughen a person up, giving her a stoic acceptance of how meat gets from the field to our table. Not me.

My grandparents lived on a small farm in Clinton, a tiny community in BC's ranching country. Over the years, they kept various animals, including goats, horses, chickens, and pigs. I remember spending one long, lazy summer with grandma and grandpa, frolicking daily with their chickens. Yes, those chick-ens really were my playmates. I would feed them dandelions. They would peck at my shoelaces until they untied them. They were so clever and had so much personality. I swore I could tell them apart.

"I'm going to play with the chickens, grandpa!" I would announce as I skipped down to their pen.

"Chickens are too dumb to play with you," he said.

He just didn't understand them. I was connecting with them on a different level.

And then, one morning, I headed to the chicken coop to see my feathered pals. To my surprise, my whole family was already there—killing them! It was like a horror movie: *The Silence of the Lambs,* except with chickens. These people I loved and trusted were slaughtering my friends and then dunking them in vats of boiling water. My own mother was participating! My sweet, loving grandma! Grandpa was behind the barn chopping their heads off (thank god I didn't have to witness that). One of my cousins came around the corner carrying a headless chicken by the feet. Its wings were still flapping. I burst into tears.

"City slicker," he hissed, seemingly enjoying my shock.

City slicker? I was from the outskirts of Quesnel (a three-hour drive north of Clinton, with a population of about twenty thousand at the time). Did having feelings and emotions and a soul make me a city slicker? If that was the case, then I was one: I was a small-town city slicker.

And then, that night, my grandma served chicken for dinner. Was she kidding me? That was crossing the line. I felt bad enough that I hadn't been able to stop the carnage. I wasn't going to compound my guilt by eating my friends.

I had barely recovered from the chicken ordeal when my parents bought a few heads of beef cattle. I was a teenager at the time, so it was my job to feed them. Every day, I tossed hay to the cows and talked to them. I even named a few of them (there were two blond ones I called Farrah Fawcett and Lee Majors). And then, a few months later:

"Mom, what's for dinner?"

"Lee Majors burgers."

On another occasion, family friends gave us some cuts of a pig that they had raised and then slaughtered. My mom made a delicious pork roast for dinner. I was happily chewing away when I felt something hard in my mouth. I spat it out on my plate. It was a bullet.

So was it any wonder I was traumatized? Reading the book *The Omnivore's Dilemma* by Michael Pollan did nothing to soothe my queasy feelings about meat. In fact, it made me long for some grandpa-killed chickens and a pork shoulder with a neighbor's humanely placed bullet in it.

The author tells tales of feedlot cattle being stuffed full of a concoction made of corn, liquefied beef tallow, protein supplements, and vitamins. Cows are meant to eat grass! Their bodies were never meant to digest all that other stuff. The diet of these feedlot cattle is so unnatural that their manure, once the perfect fertilizer for crops, has become toxic. It sits in giant manure lakes, sending methane into the atmosphere. Feedlot cattle often become very sick from this poor diet—but no matter! Let's pump them full of antibiotics before we slaughter them at the ripe old age of fourteen months.

Then Ethan came home from school one day with an announcement. "Today, the Sierra Club came to our school. They told us that the leading cause of greenhouse gas is cow breath and farts. It's true," He said, holding up one finger for emphasis. "Number one: cow farts."

"Oh my god," I said.

"Yeah," Ethan continued, "I guess we should eat more beef so we can get rid of the problem."

"Uh . . . pardon?"

"You know," he explained, "when the cow farts," (actually, he didn't say "fart," he imitated the farting noise) "it causes methane gas, which is bad for the environment. We eat the cow: no more cow farts."

"Not exactly," I said, going on to explain that eating a farting cow was not actually doing the environment a favor.

My resource books concurred with Ethan's assessment. According to *Ecoholic*, farting cows emit more greenhouse gas than cars, trains, or even planes. One hamburger patty, over the course of its life cycle, equates to driving almost six miles in your car! And feedlots are reliant on fossil fuels. *The Omnivore's Dilemma* estimated that raising one steer to a weight of twelve hundred pounds requires thirty-five gallons of oil. And *Echoholic* said that grain-fed cattle use about twelve thousand gallons of water for every pound of beef produced. It went on to say that becoming vegetarian was one of the best things you could do for the environment.

Fine by me! Given my history with animal slaughter, combined with all the new (and disgusting) information I'd learned about meat production, I would have been happy to give up meat. My husband, however, never had to watch his beloved grandmother pluck a headless chicken. John comes from a very pro-meat culture. Growing up in a household with four Australian boys, he became accustomed to meat pies on Wednesdays, steak and chips on Fridays and an enormous roast of meat on Sundays. Ethan has inherited his dad's carnivorous streak. They both simply love meat. So I decided it wasn't fair to deprive them of it completely. I made a family announcement.

"We're going to eat less meat."

"Sure," Tegan said, with an indifferent shrug.

"Why?" John and Ethan cried in unison.

"For the environment," I said, spouting off a few gory facts and frightening statistics. "Paul McCartney once said that if slaughterhouses had glass walls, we'd all be vegetarian."

"Vegetarian?" the males in my family shrieked.

"Calm down," I grumbled. "We don't have to stop eating meat completely. We're just going to go meatless a few times per week."

I watched as John pretended to scratch his eye. I think he was actually swiping at a tear. "What will we eat, then?" he pouted.

It was a good question. Mealtime had revolved around meat for so long that I hadn't many meatless meal ideas. And it wasn't that I was totally against eating meat. Because early man had been able to figure out how to hunt, it seemed that eating dead animals was "meant to be." And growing children do need protein.

I just wished meat came with a label: this steer had a lovely life with lots of fresh green grass and playtime with his friends. He had a distant but healthy relationship with his parents and was never forced to eat his own cousin. Or: this chicken was free to roam outside, pecking at bugs and shoelaces. He was not kept in a tiny cage then hung upside down by his feet waiting for his throat to be slit.

Whole Foods tries to offer such pastoral assurances. Their walls feature posters of organic farmers and ranchers with stories about their philosophies and practices. But according to

The Omnivore's Dilemma, Whole Foods rarely buys from these small farmers anymore, favoring massive industrial producers. And when author Michael Pollan checked out these supposedly humanely treated chickens and stress-free cows, he found that, in many cases, their lives were no better than their regular counterparts.

One day John came home from the grocery store with a "Happy Chicken." That's what the label said: Happy Chicken. Obviously, the chicken's joy was tempered somewhat by the fact that it was dead, but the label assured me that it had spent its life in a roomy barn with lots of natural light and room to graze and peck and play chicken tag with its friends. The chicken had been fed top-quality feed and was not given any medications. Was this just another marketing scam to make me feel better about eating a dead animal? Maybe. But we roasted the chicken and it was absolutely delicious. It was like we could taste the happiness!

When we're not eating happy chickens, we eat a lot of beans: refried beans in burritos, chickpeas in hummus, lentils in curry. And my friend Val gave me a ridiculously easy and delicious meat-free black bean soup recipe. Here it is:

RIDICULOUSLY EASY AND DELICIOUS MEAT-FREE BLACK BEAN SOUP

1 can black beans, rinsed and drained

4 cups veggie stock (or chicken stock,
but obviously then it's not entirely meat-free)

1 cup salsa

1 cup corn

Combine and heat for a few minutes. Before serving, add
a dash of hot sauce and the juice of one fresh lime. Serve
with grated cheese.

We've even learned to like tofu (all of us except Ethan, who
still manages to choke it down, probably by fantasizing that it's
a piece of steak).

I'm still confused about meat. And I still feel badly when we
eat it. Despite this guilt, we still have a meat-based meal about
four times a week. As so many of us have learned to do, I just
push my concerns to the back of my mind.

But on those nights when we have a meatless meal, I always
feel quite healthy, humane, and good to the planet. Of course,
with all the beans we're eating, our family does contribute a certain amount of methane gas to the atmosphere. But still, we're
nowhere near as bad as a whole herd of farting cattle.

Something's Fishy

• • •

WE HAD TO eat fish. It was the healthiest food on the planet. Fatty fish like salmon was full of omega–3s, which would make us smarter. And get rid of wrinkles. And fish was good for our hearts and nervous systems. And most importantly, it would get rid of wrinkles. Every time I read an interview with some gorgeous movie star, she was spouting off about how she ate nothing but salmon and broccoli for every meal. I, too, wanted to look thirty-five when I was really seventy, so I vowed to increase my fish intake.

Or maybe not. News reports screamed the warnings about fish consumption. It was filled with mercury! If you ate certain types of fish more than once a month, you'd get Alzheimer's! If your kids ate even a tiny mouthful, they'd become hyperactive and get ADD! And don't go near the stuff if you're pregnant or breastfeeding!

Then there was the ecological side of eating fish. I'd heard the horror stories about overfishing and depleted fish stocks. I'd seen economies (such as Eastern Canada's) devastated by poor management of the oceans. But what about the innocent dolphins that were slaughtered for my tuna melt? Who hadn't seen an image of a blood-red ocean as fishermen extracted their haul? And what about the use of trawling nets, which indiscriminately scoop up then discard any sea creature that happens to be in the way? Even birds and turtles fall victim to these inhumane fishing practices. All of this destruction was horrifying.

I was torn. I should eat fish if I wanted to have a healthy heart and look young, but I should avoid it if I wanted to remember my telephone number and my children's names. Plus, I didn't want to contribute to the fishing industry if it was destroying our oceans. But given my obsession with my (fading) youth, I had to have the omega–3s. As long as I chose fish that was low in mercury and responsibly caught, it would be okay. Ethan was quite the watchdog on the subject.

"Is that salmon wild?" he asked as I was making dinner one night.

"Yes."

"Good. Because farmed salmon is really bad, you know."

"I know."

There was a pause. "Why is it bad again?"

"I can't remember," I said. "Something about antibiotics."

I didn't feel like thinking about it moments before we had our fish dinner. But in the interest of making sustainable fish choices, I did some research.

Ecoholic laid it out for me simply. Farmed fish were really bad. First, they were fed pellets made of ground-up smaller fish like mackerel and anchovies. (It takes about seven pounds of wild fish to feed two pounds of farmed salmon). These little fish contain high concentrations of toxins (including dioxins, DDT, flame retardants, and hormone-disrupting PCBs). The fish pellets also include artificial colorants, because farmed fish are gray and not a lovely "salmon-pink" like wild ones.

Because farmed salmon are kept in overcrowded pens full of their own poop, they end up infested with diseases such as sea lice. Sea lice? Who knew that a hairless fish could get lice? In addition, they're stuffed with bacteria-killing antibiotics. And even in Pacific waters, fish farmers choose Atlantic salmon because they are heartier and more likely to survive than the more delicate (and tasty) Pacific varieties. *Ecoholic* said that ninety-five percent of young wild salmon that swim past an infected farm die. And what happens when these freaky, disease-resistant Atlantic salmon escape (which they do) and try to breed with our gentle (and tasty) BC fish? I didn't even want to think about it!

Obviously, the fish-farming industry was evil. And I had another, very serious issue with farmed salmon: the taste. Have you tried it? It's just so . . . fishy. When we lived in Calgary, I used to buy farmed salmon. It was all that was carried in my local grocery store. I didn't think it tasted *that* bad. The kids refused to eat it, though. They'd sit with a piece of smelly, bright-orange salmon in front of them, and no amount of cajoling would get them to put it in their mouths.

But when we got back to Vancouver, I started getting wild BC salmon from a fish market up the street. What a difference! It was red (not fluorescent orange) and so flavorful. And it didn't smell like cat food. The kids, particularly Tegan, loved it. It was healthy and delicious and not treated with any weird drugs. We could eat it all the time and be healthy and young-looking! Or could we?

I was out shopping one day when I came across a booth set up by a group called SeaChoice, an initiative of Sustainable Seafood Canada. They gave me a handy little card that would break down the fish mystery for me in a very clear, concise format. There were three categories: green, yellow, and red. Fish that were being harvested sustainably fell into the green "Best Choice" category. The yellow "Some Concerns" category was for fish whose consumption raised concerns about conservation or fishing practices. And then there was the red "Avoid" grouping of fish whose harvest caused significant habitat damage or discard of unwanted species, or whose stocks were poorly managed or endangered. There was also a little triangle next to species that posed a health threat from mercury, and a circle with a line through it for those carrying PCBS, dioxins, or pesticides.

When I got home, I decided to figure out, once and for all, the best seafood choices for my family. First, I looked for my beloved wild salmon. Obviously if it wasn't farmed, I thought, it had to be a good choice that would make my skin all dewy and youthful. I searched for it and found it . . . on the yellow "Some Concerns" list! What? Even wild Pacific salmon was a choice with some concerns? There were two little asterisks beside it, suggesting that I go online to check the salmon recommendations seasonally. I don't know about you, but I don't give dinner that much forethought.

If wild salmon wasn't a great choice, then what was? I looked at the green section to see what kind of fish we should be eating. First on the list: US-farmed catfish. Yum, my favorite! (I'm being sarcastic, in case you couldn't tell.) While farmed catfish may very well be delicious and healthy, it's not exactly something I'm likely to cook at home (I don't eat fish with whiskers). Next on the list was farmed sturgeon caviar, followed by farmed clams, farmed tilapia, Pacific hake, and herring (it didn't specify whether the last two should be wild or farmed)—none of which I had ever included on my dinner menu. There were farmed mussels, oysters, pollock, and US sardines. Pacific cod was a good choice, but only if it was caught by bottom longline, jig, or pot. Swordfish was also a sustainable choice if it was harpooned in Atlantic Canada.

I scrolled the best-choice list for fish I had actually eaten before and would consider eating again. Farmed rainbow trout was on the list. I had at least tried trout before—when I went camping as a kid. And sidestripe or spot prawns were a great local choice (if they were trap caught).

And then I found it. It was the last item on the list: tuna! Hooray! Tuna was a sustainable seafood choice—if it was albacore, bigeye, skipjack, or yellowfin—not bluefin. And the correct type of tuna had to be troll-caught. Then I noticed a small black diamond beside the word tuna, which meant that there were high levels of mercury in all types of tuna. So did that mean tuna was a sustainable, but slightly poisonous, choice for lunch?

Looking through the choices, I found tuna on the yellow "Some Concerns" list, too. If tuna was caught by pelagic longline in US waters it wasn't quite as good a choice. (Pelagic longline is a method of fishing where a long line baited with hundreds, even thousands, of hooks is dragged across the surface of the water. While it works well for catching tuna, it also catches seabirds, turtles, and other fish.) And there was a little black mercury triangle next to this tuna, too.

I also found tuna on the red "Avoid" list. Tuna caught in Pacific *international* waters by pelagic longline should be avoided, as should all bluefin tuna. This giant species has been fished to the brink of extinction thanks, in large part, to sport fishermen wanting to "bag a big one" and, therefore, compensate for their small penises.

I suddenly noticed a pattern. While farmed caviar was on the "Best Choice" list, wild caviar was under the "Avoid" heading. Clams hit all three categories (farmed were good, Atlantic soft-shell clams and wild Pacific geoduck had some concerns, and dredged Atlantic clams should be avoided). Crab, too, was on all three lists. Dungeness was a good choice, if you ignored the little mercury triangle; king and snow crab didn't have a mercury triangle but had some sustainability issues; and king crab from Russia was to be avoided at all costs. Farmed mussels were good; wild mussels less so.

So the same fish could be a good, okay, or bad choice, depending on what species it was and where and how it was caught. I hurried to my cupboard and picked up a can of tuna, figuring that all the information I needed should have been printed right on the label.

Some of it was. My tuna was Ocean's yellowfin chunk light tuna in water. Yellowfin was one of the good kinds. But mine was imported from Thailand. Uh-oh. That would qualify as international waters, right? Tuna caught by pelagic longline in international waters was a bad choice. But there was a little "Dolphin Friendly" symbol, so maybe it was okay? I searched the label to find how the fish had been caught. I needed it to be troll caught, please be troll caught. I ripped the label off and read the reverse side. There were the caloric, cholesterol, and sodium contents, but nothing about the fishing method.

But the label did have a Web site: www.oceanfish.com. I checked it out. To my surprise, I found that Ocean Fisheries, Ltd. was situated in Richmond, BC, not far from my home. They caught only wild salmon off the coast of British Columbia and Alaska, and supported responsible, sustainable fisheries-management practices. Their site said that they looked at the whole ecosystem, going beyond commercially targeted species and their habitat and fully participating with the government, fishers, First Nations, coastal communities, and conservation groups to develop responsible management plans.

Cool. But what about the tuna? While I didn't find the term "troll caught," I did find clarification on their "Dolphin Friendly" sticker. It said that, since 1991, Ocean Fisheries, Ltd. has not harmed dolphins or other marine mammals as they fish, and has been leading the way in environmental responsibility. They don't buy tuna from vessels that net fish associated with dolphins, or tuna caught with gill nets or drift nets, since these can sometimes entrap dolphins, other marine animals, or birds. They require certification of dolphin-safe fishing practices from all their tuna suppliers. It also said that their dolphin-friendly policy has been certified by Earth Island Institute's International Marine Mammal Project.

So it sounded like my yellowfin tuna was a good environmental choice. But nothing is that simple when we're talking about sustainable seafood. The following day, I received my *FOCUS* newsletter from the World Wildlife Fund. In their January/February 2008 issue, there was an article saying that the world's first sustainable tuna fishery had just been certified. The world's first? Did that mean that the fishery where Ocean's got their tuna was not sustainable? The Marine Stewardship Council (MSC) had certified a small, family-run fishery that caught tuna using poles and barbless hooks, landing fish one at a time. Of course, this tuna was not available everywhere (Whole Foods might have it) and was, understandably, more expensive.

Oh well, I didn't like the look of that little black mercury triangle anyway. I went online and found a consumption advisory chart on the Environmental Defense Fund's Web site (www.edf.org). It said that adults can safely consume white, canned tuna three times a month. An older child (aged six to twelve) can safely have it twice per month, and a child under six can only eat it once every thirty days. So what would happen if you ate it more than that? Cancer? Alzheimer's? Toxic mercury poisoning that makes your hair fall out and oozing lesions pop up all over your body? What if I gave my kids tuna sandwiches for lunch yesterday and today, and then on the weekend, they went to a friend's house and unwittingly ate a third tuna sandwich? What then? So I decided to go off tuna. There were still three cans left in our cupboard, but once they were gone (which would take four to five months, to be on the safe side), I would stop buying it.

But luckily, canned tuna was not our only seafood option. We live on the coast. Fresh, sustainably caught fish should be plentiful and affordable. And there was an excellent fish store a few blocks away. The staff were mostly young Australian guys who were trying to earn money to go snowboarding every spare minute of their lives, but they really seemed to know a lot about fish. And they were so cute and friendly! They even sort of flirted with me as I ordered my wild salmon tails (there are fewer bones in the tails, a cute young Australian guy informed me).

Okay, they probably weren't flirting with me. I probably reminded them of their mother back home, or perhaps a young-ish aunt. Anyway, they were a helpful bunch, and I felt confident that they could help me solve my fish dilemma.

So I strolled into the fish store with confidence, trying to ignore the smell and the freezing temperature. I took a number and waited as several other patrons made their fish selections. The store was always busy, due to the freshness of the fish and, possibly, the cuteness of the staff.

"Number twenty-eight!" a young Australian guy called. That was me. I hurried forward.

"Can I help you?" he asked in his cute Australian accent.

"I hope so." I smiled at him. "Can you tell me where this halibut was caught?"

"Off the Queen Charlotte Islands," he replied, his eyes twinkling at me.

See? I knew they were knowledgeable as well as adorable. "Great! Can you tell me if it was caught by bottom longline?"

He looked at me like I was speaking Portuguese. "Sorry?"

"Was the halibut caught using bottom longline?"

"Uh . . ." He gestured toward the back. "I could go look it up for you?"

I looked at the line up of people waiting behind me. "Hurry up you tree-hugging environmental zealot," I could hear them thinking. Or, "Quit monopolizing the cute Aussie boy. It's my turn to flirt with him."

"Don't worry about it," I said. "I'll take that piece there."

The confusion was too much. In fact, it practically turned me off eating fish altogether. But unfortunately, the confusion did nothing to quell my vanity—or my jittery constitution. My skin and nerves needed the omega–3s! I decided to take fish oil capsules.

I know there's a whole school of thought that says popping a pill isn't the same as getting the nutrients from eating the actual food. But these capsules aren't full of some chemical concoction. They're full of oil squeezed out of sardines (a "Best Choice") and anchovies (which, for some reason, are not on the card at all). I have no idea how they're caught, or if it even matters, but the label on the bottle assures me that they are free of mercury and PCBs. So I'm sorry, little anchovies and sardines, for eating your oil. But what am I supposed to do? Fish is just too damned complicated. And I'm at an age where skin care has become extremely important.

What's the Deal with Dairy?

• • •

MILK IS A staple of virtually every growing child's diet. "Drink your milk," our mothers always said. "It'll make you grow up big and strong." And I did drink my milk. And I did grow up big and strong. So obviously it made sense to pour the stuff down my children's gullets, as well. Or did it? While Canada's Food Guide and conventional dieticians still dictate that dairy products build strong bones and teeth, this pure-white, healthy drink now swirls with controversy.

My first inkling that maybe dairy products weren't foods of the gods came when I was in my early twenties. I was working for the telephone company and often went to a nearby food court for lunch with a group of coworkers. I had just ordered a slice of three-cheese pizza with extra cheese, when my coworker Kevin mentioned that he didn't eat dairy

"Why not?" I asked, biting into a mouthful of mozzarella, Romano, and Parmesan.

"Because drinking the milk of another species is wrong and disgusting and bad for you," he replied.

"Oh . . ."

Kevin elaborated. "Cow's milk is meant to nourish a calf, not a human. Its nutritional makeup is specifically bovine, so it can cause all sorts of health problems in people—superfluous mucus, cancer, heart disease, bad breath . . ."

Oh god! If Kevin was right, dairy products were gross and dangerous. But I doubted Kevin knew what he was talking about. He'd always seemed like a bit of a paranoid, hypochondriac type. And how could I ignore all those print ads with our favorite celebrities wearing milk-mustaches or flaunting their perfectly toned bodies above the caption: "Milk, It Does a Body Good"? Surely the advertisers wouldn't *lie* to us, would they? I put Kevin's words out of my mind. Even if it was true, I wasn't ready to hear it. I was involved in a passionate love affair with cheese, and no amount of scaremongering was going to drive me from it.

Years later, the rumblings about the evils of milk had increased. Or maybe I was just listening now because I had children. It wasn't just me the cheese could be killing, it was my precious offspring. I stumbled upon Web sites, like notmilk. com and milksucks.com, devoted to the evils of dairy products. There was even a book called *Milk—The Deadly Poison*. All three sources purported that milk was unhealthy, cruel to animals, and terrible for the environment.

But was that really the truth? And if it was, could I handle the truth? Because, despite my concerns about hormones, antibiotics, and inhumane dairy farms, I was still severely addicted to cheese. Cheese was my crack cocaine. I didn't care if it made my breath bad or caused mucus buildup or if the nutrients in it were tailor-made for a baby cow. I was even willing to risk the myriad of diseases dairy products were said to cause. Cheese was worth it. I couldn't live without it—although I had, once, back in 2004. It was the longest five weeks of my life.

It all started with a visit to a naturopath. It was just after our momentous move from Calgary to Australia and back to Vancouver within one year. My first book had just come out, and I was feeling really stressed-out and overwhelmed. Instead of going to my doctor for a prescription of Valium, I decided to go the alternative route. I was hoping for some kind of calming herbal concoction (like the valerian–Saint-John's-wort cocktail I'd had in Australia). Instead, this naturopath suggested I get tested for "food sensitivities."

"Sure," I said, naïvely assuming that I might be sensitive to, say, turmeric or pickled herring. No. According to her tests, I was sensitive to wheat, dairy, sugar, alcohol, caffeine, chocolate, corn, peanuts, aspergillus (an additive in soy sauce), and fava beans. Okay, the aspergillus and fava beans I could work around, but the rest of it? It was like some kind of sick torture! Why not just ban sex, movies, and hugging my children? What was the point of living?

"You'll feel so much better that you'll never go back to eating those banned foods again," my naturopath assured me.

My best friend, who had had a vegan stint, echoed her senti-ment. "The whites of your eyes will be so white!" she said.

I'd never noticed that the whites of my eyes were particu-larly dingy. But I was very stressed-out and run-down, so maybe it was worth a try. If I put my mind to it, I could eliminate those foods from my diet. When I was feeling calm and energized and my eyeball whites were glowing, it would all be worth it.

It was surprising how many "replacement" foods were avail-able. If you don't eat wheat, you can eat rice pasta and rye bread. You can use rice flour for baking and replace sugar with honey or maple syrup. And soy milk is fine on cereal or in tea. But there is no replacement for cheese. (There's no replacement for choco-late or red wine, either, but we're talking about cheese here.)

Well, there is a replacement for cheese. It's called soy cheese. It tastes like eating a rubber flip-flop—after it's had a bare foot in it for three months—except the flip-flop would actually have more flavor. This is just my opinion. I suppose there is someone out there who loves soy cheese. No, there can't be. It's horrible.

After five long weeks on my restricted diet, I took stock. How did I feel? Not bad. How hard was it to stick to this eating plan? Hard, but considerably easier than when I first started. How white were the whites of my eyes? No noticeable differ-ence. I decided then that it wasn't worth it. I enjoyed food too much. I missed cheese. (I missed wine and chocolate too, but this is about cheese.) That was probably the last cheese-free day of my life.

But ever since that diet, I had gotten out of the habit of drinking milk. I didn't miss it, so I didn't see the need to go back. But I was still giving it to my kids at every meal. Was it really as bad as many natural health care practitioners were saying? And what was its impact on the environment? I couldn't bury my head in the sand (or in a pile of Parmesan cheese) any longer. I had to find out.

First, I researched the claims regarding hormones and antibiotics in milk. *Ecoholic* said that, in Canada, bovine growth hormones used to boost milk production are illegal. Yay! But they are used in the United States. Boo! Antibiotics are legal for use on dairy cattle in Canada, but the milk has to test below certain residue levels before it can be sold to consumers. So that's good . . . sort of . . . I think. Antibiotic use is crucial to the milk industry because cow teats often become infected from overuse. Yes, *infected*. That means there could be pus and blood in the milk I'm feeding my kids (but at least it's pasteurized).

Ecoholic also expounded on the environmental impact of the dairy industry. Dairy cows poop—a lot. That manure has to be stored somewhere, usually in open piles on the ground or in unlined lagoons. These methods lead to poop runoff, which pollutes groundwater, rivers, and streams.

And much like their beef-cattle relatives, dairy cows do not have very nice lives. PETA's Web site milksucks.com was all too happy to lay out the horror stories for me. It said that huge milk factories use genetic manipulation and intensive production technologies so that dairy cows can produce one hundred pounds of milk a day. That's ten times more than they would naturally. The factories also use growth hormones and accelerated milking schedules. These can cause the dairy cows' udders to become so heavy that they sometimes drag on the ground, resulting in frequent infections that require antibiotics.

And let's not forget the calves, the "byproducts" of the dairy industry. Milksucks.com said that dairy cows are artificially inseminated every year. (We can't even offer them the pleasure of getting pregnant the old-fashioned way? Although . . . maybe cow sex is not all that pleasurable.) Male calves are often kept in cramped veal crates for fourteen to seventeen weeks before they are slaughtered. Female calves usually grow up to be "milk machines" like their mothers.

Good grief! It was horrific. Maybe organic milk was a better option? But even that was prone to controversy. *Ecoholic* said that organic dairy farmers had been accused of having lax standards to keep prices low and quantities up. It went on to say that vague and poorly enforced standards could mean that organic dairy cows are not allowed adequate time to graze outside, and even organic farms can resemble factory feedlots. Not to mention that organic milk costs a small fortune (in Vancouver, $5.99 for a half gallon compared to $3.49 for a half gallon of conventional milk).

One of my Kitsilano friends fed her kids organic goats' milk supplied by a local Abbotsford farm. The farm's Web site stated that they used no hormones, rarely used antibiotics, and treated their goats with love and kindness. The goats lived in spacious barns with access to outdoor pastures. And it stands to reason that goats would be better for the environment, too. Just look at a tiny goat-poo pellet versus an enormous cow plop. Goats' milk has health benefits, too. It is easier to digest than cows' milk (something to do with smaller fat globules). It seemed a perfect solution.

"It's not cheap," my friend said, "but it's worth it."

"How not cheap is it?" I asked.

"About fifteen dollars a gallon. We go through a couple of gallons a week."

Jesus Murphy! Thirty bucks a week for milk?! I'd have to sell a kidney—or some other expendable organ. Are there other expendable organs? Organic goats' milk was the champagne of milk. I simply couldn't afford it.

Soy milk was a more affordable option, but I'd seen a news report that said soy crops were one of the main contributors to the devastation of the rain forest (though much of that soy was fed to beef cattle). A lot of soy milk was genetically modified and it was also full of sugar. (Why add sugar? It still tastes like crap.) Rice milk was another alternative, but it was full of oil. And just because it was white didn't make it milk. It was rice juice!

I was at a loss. I now knew that cows' milk was gross and mean to cows and bad for the environment. But on the other side of the coin, it was affordable and Ethan loved it. And I still remember having serious milk cravings when I was growing up. I would drink glass after glass of the stuff. Maybe a child's growing body needs that baby-cow calcium? And then there was the whole cheese issue. I was an addict and I wasn't ready to give it up. I hadn't reached my cheese-addiction rock bottom yet.

Ethan and I discussed the subject when we were walking home from school one day. Since he was the biggest milk consumer in the household, I thought I should get his input. When

I'd filled him in on the whole gloomy picture, he said, "Maybe we could buy our own cow?"

I suppose that would have been the kindest, most environmentally friendly approach but: "No." (To be honest, after about two days of getting up at six AM to milk the thing then shoveling cow pies out of the backyard, I don't know if I'd be that kind to it anyway.)

"Well," my son suggested, "could we just buy milk from a farm where they're actually nice to the cows?"

I pondered that for a moment. "I'm not sure such a place exists," I said ruefully. But maybe such a place did exist. And maybe it was right in my own backyard?

I had always noticed the glass bottles of milk perched next to the enormous plastic jugs I was buying. There was something so old-fashioned, so wholesome about those bottles. Was it just because they conjured images of a fifties milkman, dressed in white, delivering milk to a Cleaver-esque family? Or could this milk really be a better alternative? I decided to look into it.

The company's Web site said that the dairy farm began in 1906, in the south of Vancouver. Over a hundred years later, it is still a family-run business. In the last few years, it has moved toward organic farming, producing milk without antibiotics, hormones, or pesticides. The site touted the benefits of organic milk: it was produced without GMOs and contained no artificial colors or preservatives. And animal welfare was always foremost on the farmers' minds. The company's organic dairy cows had access to the outdoors, fresh air, pure water, sunshine, and exercise.

But what about the conventional side of their operation? I'd already determined that organic milk was too expensive. I knew the conventional cows would be ingesting some pesticides and antibiotics (I guess I was willing to drink a few contaminants to keep from having to sell one kidney and my spleen), but how were the non-organic animals treated? Did the farmer care about their welfare, too? Or did the organic cows get to hang out in the field, eating green grass and soaking up rays while the regular cows were stuck in a crappy factory with their udders dragging on the floor? I had to know! I decided to e-mail the dairy.

> *Dear Sir or Madam,*
> *I saw on your site that your organic cows have access to the outdoors, fresh air, pure water, sunshine, and exercise. Do your conventional cows have the same?*
> *Thank you very much,*
> *Concerned for Cows*

The representative wrote back within a day or two.

> *Dear Concerned for Cows,*
> *The conventional cows do go outside, however not for a specific amount of time. Some days they may go out for eight hours, some for sixteen. The organic cows must go outside for a minimum of 16 hours a day. Their water is filtered 3 times, prior to them consuming it. The conventional cows get regular water from a tap.*

Tap water? Could I allow my family to drink the milk of an animal that ingested *tap water?* Of course I could! And these cows got to go outside and eat grass and enjoy the sun (or more often the rain, since they were Vancouver cows). I decided to do it. I was going to switch to this company's products.

The milk cost about fifty cents more per quart, but the peace of mind was well worth it. Plus, I loved the glass bottles. Given all the controversy surrounding plastic food containers, I was happy to pay the dollar deposit and return my bottles for reuse. The kids seemed to find the glass bottles a novelty and insisted the milk tasted so much better.

The dairy celebrated its hundredth anniversary in 2006, and I came across a *Vancouver Sun* article about the festivities. The writer finished up his story by saying that when Queen Elizabeth comes to Vancouver, she will drink only standard, unhomogenized (that's the kind where the cream still rises to the top) milk from this dairy. Maybe it wasn't organic goats' milk, but if it was good enough for Liz, it was surely good enough for us.

Our Largest Organ

· · ·

I **WAS PRETTY SATISFIED** with what my family and I were putting into our bodies. Sure, we could have gone hard-core vegetarian, hard-core organic, and hard-core local. But we weren't really hard-core kind of people. I felt I'd reached a pretty good compromise when it came to consumables. We were eating mostly healthy, environmentally friendly foods. I had done my research and I was making informed choices. If, god forbid, we did get some kind of freaky hormone or pesticide-related tumor, it wouldn't be for lack of caution.

Then Ethan brought home a science worksheet from school. They were studying the human body.

"What's the biggest organ in our bodies?" he quizzed me.

"Oh! I know this one! Uh . . . the liver?"

"Wrong. It's the skin. The skin disposes of waste, protects vital organs, and regulates body temperature."

"Right," I said. "I actually knew that, I just forgot. Yeah, the skin . . ."

I had known that at one time (probably in fifth grade). I actually remember thinking, "Wow, I never thought of my skin as an organ before. I thought of it as well . . . skin." Not that I didn't consider skin important. It was ultra-important! I slathered myself in all sorts of lotions and oils to keep my largest organ soft and smooth and young-looking. I washed my largest organ with moisturizing soaps and body washes, buffing it with exfoliating scrubs to remove dead skin cells. When the kids came along, I coated their every crack and crevice (well, their major crack and crevice) with petroleum jelly or diaper-rash cream to protect them from irritations. So even if I hadn't considered the skin an organ, I'd been treating it very well for years.

That's when my friend Deb told me about a British celebrity's line of skin-care products. "It's all organic and free of chemicals and stuff," she said.

"But does it work?" I countered. "Don't we need all those chemicals and stuff to be soft and smooth and young-looking?"

"Apparently not," she said. "This celebrity believes that what you put *on* your body is just as important as what you put in it."

"That's a bit much," I scoffed. This celeb obviously qualified as hard core about her health and that of the planet, whereas I did not. I was committed to doing my best, but I wasn't going to go over the top. Still, I went to her Web site.

The slogan for her skin-care product line was: "Everything Your Skin Needs, and Nothing It Doesn't." All products were produced with one hundred percent organic active ingredients and absolutely no chemical preservatives, petrochemicals, or silicones.

I liked the idea of using all-natural skin-care products, but did it really matter? Would rubbing preservatives, petrochemicals, and silicones on our bodies give us cancer? Would pouring them down the drain kill fish and wildlife? And if we then ate that fish or wildlife, would we get Alzheimer's? Surely, if all-natural and organic skin care was that important, I would have heard something about it by now. I still wasn't convinced. Luckily, I didn't have to give it too much thought. Thanks to the premium pricing of this organic skin-care line, only rich people like Madonna and Gwyneth Paltrow could afford to worry about chemicals in their moisturizer.

But then I started to hear about it . . . a lot. Of course it mattered what we put on our skin, experts said on the news and in magazines. It was our biggest organ, after all! Even some of my friends were getting on board. Deb had splurged on some natural and organic potions, and her skin looked really good. When our water heater broke and I had to shower at a neighbor's house, I noticed that her bathroom was full of organic skin-care prod-, ucts, too. Was I missing the boat?

Then Oprah did an episode on natural skin care. God, even Oprah was on board! (And when Oprah's on board, you know that you'd better get on board fast or you'll be the last person left standing on the dock.) Her special guests that day were

Julia Roberts and a pretty blond woman who knew everything there was to know about being "gorgeously green." Her name was Sophie Uliano, and she'd written a book with that very title: *Gorgeously Green*, published in 2008. She and Julia went on to talk about all the deadly chemicals in everything from baby food to shampoos, from nail polish to deodorant (by the way, Julia Roberts does not wear deodorant and, according to Oprah, smells absolutely lovely).

"Chuck out anything that contains fragrance or parfum," Sophie said, "Or triclosan or aluminum."

Julia laughed and said something like, "I threw out every product in my bathroom and half my kitchen."

But I didn't want to throw out hundreds of dollars worth of skin- and hair-care products. That was really wasteful— and expensive! And if these products were so highly toxic, was throwing them away the best answer? Shouldn't they be taken to some hazardous material site for proper disposal? Where was the Vancouver haz-mat dump? I didn't even know. I felt slightly sick and overwhelmed. Were all my efforts to feed my family healthy food for naught because I allowed them to rub carcinogens all over their largest organs? Damn it!

Although I wasn't quite ready to throw out all my lotions and shampoos, I decided to supplement them with some natural skin-care products. When I was buying groceries at our locally owned natural grocery store, I purchased some body lotion. "Obsessively natural," the slogan said. Perfect! I bought a bar of soap from the same line. A few days later, I went to get my hair cut. At the salon, I purchased bottles of shampoo and conditioner from a well-known company that uses natural plant and flower essences. Sure, my new products cost about double the price of my old, cancer-causing products, but it was worth the peace of mind.

About two weeks later, I went to school to pick up my kids. One of the school moms approached me. "Have you read this book?" she said, removing it from her reusable shopping bag. There it was: *Gorgeously Green.*

"No, but I saw the author on Oprah," I said. (This is a disturbingly frequent response of mine.)

"It's really eye-opening," she continued. "Did you know that only eleven percent of the ingredients in beauty products have been tested for safety?

Valerie Green approached. "I did," she said. "I mean, we all know about the parabens and phthalates, but there are all sorts of other nasty chemicals in skin care and makeup, and who knows what they do."

"I've got to go," I mumbled. Maybe using up my old, chemical-filled products wasn't good enough? I hurried to the bookstore and bought *Gorgeously Green.*

The book promised "8 Simple Steps to an Earth-Friendly Life." It was a comprehensive guide to becoming a healthier, fitter, greener citizen of the planet. But I was already quite green and fit. I just wanted to know what deadly chemicals were in my hand lotion. I flicked directly to chapter two, which was all about identifying the toxic substances in your beauty products and finding green ways to take care of your skin.

Sophie Uliano reiterated what Ethan had learned in science

class. The skin is the largest organ in the body and absorbs everything you put on it. While food has to travel through the digestive system before it is absorbed into your body, the chemicals you apply to your skin are absorbed directly into the bloodstream. So maybe what you put on your body is even *more* important than what you put in it?

The book suggested that you grab all your skin- and hair-care products and put them on the kitchen table. You then look at the ingredients and sort the products into three groups: chuck out immediately or you will drop dead by the end of the year (it didn't really say the last part but I felt it was implied), finish but don't buy again (which had been my initial strategy), and investigate further.

So I gathered up all our shampoos, conditioners, lotions, soaps, facial washes, and toothpaste and marched into the kitchen. "Kids, we're going to play a game," I said.

"What kind of game?" Tegan asked.

"It's called: find the deadly chemicals that will kill us in our skin- and hair-care products."

"Fun!" Ethan said, with a healthy dose of sarcasm.

"Okay," I said, "we're looking for the worst ingredients: coal tar, fragrance, hydroquinone, aluminum, triclosan, p-Phenylene-diamine, lead, and mercury.

"Well," Ethan said, picking up a bottle of lotion, "this one has *phenalthmlmlmlmixxzzzz* and *sodium sufflemufflewuffle*."

"Right . . . What about aluminum? Or triclosan?"

"Uh . . . it does have *glickerel sulfulufullate* . . . and *oleekonium chloride*."

"I think those are fine," I said, scanning the ingredients in our hand lotion. "Ah ha!" I cried. "Our hand lotion has deadly fragrance in it!"

"So should we chuck it out?" Tegan asked.

I guess we should have. It had one of the top-five worst ingredients in it. But it only had *one* of the top-five worst ingredients in it. And there was so much left. It just seemed so wasteful. Couldn't it go into the "use but don't buy again" pile? "Umm . . . let's just set it aside for now."

"This game is kind of boring," Tegan said.

Boy, was it ever. Reading all the chemical names was making my head ache. And I hadn't even gotten to the orange-alert list with common ingredients like cocamide DEA, lauramide DEA, triethanolamine, and diethanolamine. And then there were the parabens, the phthalates, and sodium lauryl sulfate!

Thankfully, my friend had sent me a link to the Environmental Working Group's cosmetic safety database. *Gorgeously Green* also touted the nonprofit group as an expert source on what products are and are not safe to use on your body and praised their efforts to pressure companies to make the world a healthier place. I went to the Web site at www.cosmeticsdatabase.com.

It was so easy! All I had to do was type in the name of my product, and the site would give it a ranking. A rank of zero through two meant the product was a low hazard, three through six meant moderate hazard, and if you used products ranked seven through ten you'd be dead by the end of the year (just kidding). The site also provided a checklist.

Ingredients used by this brand have been linked to:

✓ Cancer

✓ Developmental/reproductive toxicity

✓ Violations, restrictions and warnings

✓ Allergies/immunotoxicity

✓ Other concerns [such as] Neurotoxicity . . . Organ system toxicity . . . Irritation (skin, eyes, or lungs), Enhanced skin absorption, etc.

This was going to be so much fun!

I began punching in my products. My regular shampoo got a rating of five (Sophie Uliano recommended not using anything with a rating of five or higher). Thank god I'd bought that new, expensive salon shampoo. It was sure to score better than a five. I entered it in the database. Five! What? I felt so disappointed. And ripped off. I entered my new natural soap bar in the database. It got a three. So did my old, cheap, toxic cancer soap. Were these pricey, so-called natural products no better than cheap drugstore brands full of chemicals?

It was time to check the body lotion I'd been slathering all over myself and my children for years. It got an eight. An eight! I knew it had red-alert fragrance in it, but an eight? We were going to be dead by the end of the year! Thankfully, the new natural lotion I bought got a four.

I'll admit to getting a little obsessed with this database. I punched every product I had, or had ever had, into it. My deodorant got a three. My toothpaste was a four. When I visited friends and relatives, I'd take note of their products and punch them in. "Wow," I'd say to John. "I can't believe your nanna is still alive at ninety-nine, and she's been using a soap with a five rating!"

The Environmental Working Group (EWG) had also produced a report on sunscreen. Thank god! I'd been increasingly confused about the stuff. A few years ago, my doctor had been concerned about the sun spots I had on my skin. She'd sent me to a dermatologist.

He quickly glanced over my naked body. "Everything's normal," he said, "but never set foot outside again without wearing SPF 75 or you will get melanoma and die within the year."

I followed his instructions—for a while, anyway. But then I started to hear conflicting information. Maybe the sun wasn't the deadly fireball we all thought it was? In fact, avoiding the sun had led to high rates of vitamin-D deficiency in North America. According to canada.com's news service, up to sixty percent of the North American population had low levels of vitamin D. And, according to a June 2008 report in the journal *Archives of Internal Medicine*, low levels of vitamin D "can be considered a strong risk indicator for all-cause mortality in women and in men." "All-cause mortality"? So you were more likely to die from *anything* if you were vitamin-D deficient? I doubt that included sky diving accidents and shark attacks, but still!

In *Gorgeously Green*, Sophie Uliano cited the overuse of sunscreen as contributing to this rampant D deficiency. She said that most doctors recommend ten to fifteen minutes of full sun a day, with no sunscreen. In Vancouver, it's simply not possible to get that much sunshine. The sun only shines for about ten to fifteen minutes all winter!

But, according to the EWG, the sun was still a deadly fireball, and sunscreen was imperative. More than a million people in the U.S. are diagnosed with skin cancer every year, with that number steadily rising over the past ten years. Given the dire predictions of that scary dermatologist, I wasn't going to take any chances. I had to wear sunscreen. And my poor kids were probably going to inherit my sun-spotty skin, so they did too. The question was: which sunscreen should we choose?

The EWG's Web site pronounced that four out of five sunscreens contained chemicals that may pose health hazards or don't adequately protect skin from the sun's damaging rays. And leading brands were some of the worst culprits. Fortunately, the EWG had compiled a list of the best sunscreens. Unfortunately, I couldn't find many of those brands at my local drugstore or health food store.

I printed out the EWG's handy shopper's guide. It recommended avoiding products that contain oxybenzone or benzophenone-3, as these chemicals can cause allergies and hormonal problems. Fragrance, as I already knew, was very very bad, as was sunscreen with bug repellent (chemical overdose!). Spray and powder sunscreens were a big no-no, as inhaling sunscreen chemicals is not a good idea. Many popular brands were not recommended because fewer than five percent of their products were considered safe and effective.

What you did want in your sunscreen was at least seven percent zinc oxide or titanium dioxide for broad-spectrum (both UVA and UVB) protection. You also needed SPF 30 or higher or there wasn't much point. The guide suggested buying new sunscreen each year (I think I was still using leftover stuff from 1998).

So I went to my local drugstore and found a sunscreen that fit the bill. It was a "sensitive skin" sunblock on the recommended list (even though the brand itself wasn't really recommended). I bought a bottle and slathered it all over myself and my kids. I felt good. We were protected from the sun's damaging UVA and UVB rays, without coating ourselves in deadly chemicals. Now, I just had to hope we didn't die of something caused by vitamin-D deficiency.

The New
Boogeyman

• • •

THE **SKIN-CARE PRODUCTS** fiasco had been the last straw. I was now certified "enviro-mental." I was still a fully functioning member of society, but deep down, I was confused (about food choices), guilt-ridden (that I wasn't doing enough to be green), and stressed-out (that people were judging my efforts). At least as a working mom I was used to living with a certain level of anxiety. But I wondered how this whole environmental thing was affecting my children.

It's impossible to shelter kids from the harsh realities of climate change. The news regularly features some horrific hurricane or cyclone that is attributed to the warming of the earth. Movie stars make documentaries about the environmental crisis. Newspaper headlines scream stuff like "Global Warming Will Kill Us All!" With these media saturation levels, even Amish children know that the planet is in a precarious state.

When I was a kid, I was a big worrier. At night, I would lie in my bunk bed with the pink gingham curtains and obsess over the state of the world. I didn't have to worry about the ice caps melting or what kind of hormones were in my food or whether a hurricane might destroy my city or some really great tourist destination. I was more concerned about war—nuclear war in particular. It was the seventies, and the Cold War was all over the news. Somewhere, I had heard about "the button," and I spent countless hours obsessing about it. What did it look like? Was it red? It would have to be red, wouldn't it? Did it have one of those acrylic cases around it, or was it just sitting right out there in the open? My mom would come in to check on me and find me lying there, eyes wide open with fear of the impending apocalypse.

"Will there be a nuclear war?" I would ask.

"No, of course not," she'd say, reassuringly.

"How do you know?"

"Well . . . I don't know for sure, but I'm quite certain there won't be."

"Yeah, but what if that Russian guy with his finger on the button gets so mad that he just decides to blow up the world? Or what if he slips? What if he's reaching for a tissue and he accidentally—"

"Look," my mom would interrupt me, trying to contain her frustration, "an eight-year-old girl should not be worrying about nuclear war. Stop thinking about it and go to sleep."

"Okay," I'd mumble, as she kissed my cheek and prepared to exit. "Mom?" I would call, just as she reached the door. "Will I get a brain tumor?"

Unfortunately, it appears that worrying may be genetic. While researchers don't seem to care enough to study this link, I have evidence that fretting is hereditary. Both my kids worry— though not to the debilitating, sleep-depriving levels that I did. But who can blame them? There are so many things to worry about! There are still wars and brain tumors. And now, we can add global warming to the "boogeyman" list.

Ethan, in particular, has an innate ability to latch onto a subject and not let it go (see chapter seven). A couple of summers ago, we were driving in the car and it started to rain. As the drops splattered on the windshield, he asked, "Could that be acid rain?"

"What?" Tegan shrieked. "Rain that is *acid?*"

"No, it's not," I assured them.

"We could test it," my son suggested. "We saw a video at school. You just have to put a glass of cabbage juice outside. If it turns red, it's acid rain."

If only I'd been drinking a tall, frothy glass of cabbage juice, it would have been so easy to allay their fears. Instead, I had to explain that acid rain was more of an Eastern problem caused by large polluting factories. This seemed to appease them and they dropped the subject . . . for the moment. But other environmental concerns (Will Vancouver be under water when the ice caps melt? Will polar bears become extinct?) have surfaced again and again.

I wasn't sure how to address these issues with my kids. Obviously, the future of the planet rested on their narrow shoulders. But if I told them too much, would it give them nightmares? Cause depression and anxiety? I'm pretty sure it would have done in me. But I couldn't just shove the subject under the rug and let them grow up eating off paper plates and saving up to buy their first Hummer.

I thought maybe Queen Latifah could do a better job than I could. On Friday, our family movie night, I rented *Arctic Tale*. It's a *National Geographic* documentary, narrated by the "Queen," that follows the lives of a polar bear cub and a walrus pup as they try to survive in the rapidly melting Arctic. My girlfriend Pam had watched it with her kids and said it was an excellent, age-appropriate movie with a strong message about caring for the environment. Perfect.

"Hey kids," I said, when I returned home from the video store. "I got us *Arctic Tale*."

"Ohhhhh," Ethan said, disappointment written all over his face. "I was hoping we could watch *Aliens vs. Predator: Requiem*."

"Forget it. That's a violent horror movie. It's rated R."

As usual, he threw the one R-rated movie I'd let him watch in his lifetime back in my face. "You let me watch *Terminator*, remember? It's rated R."

"An R-rated movie from the eighties is not the same as an R-rated movie today," I grumbled. "We're watching a movie about cute little animals dying and that's that."

We settled down with our bowls of popcorn and started the movie. As the credits rolled, I thought I should give the kids a heads-up. "Pam watched this and said it's a little sad," I explained. "Some of these animals may die."

"Okay." My son nodded bravely, but Tegan looked up at me.

"Will any polar bears die?" she asked anxiously.

"Maybe," I said, patting her little hand. "But in nature, life is hard. And sometimes animals don't survive."

"But Knut lives in a zoo," she said, referring to the baby polar bear who was the star of the Berlin zoo. At school, Tegan had read the story of Knut. He had been rejected by his mother, so was raised by a caring zookeeper. We'd spent significant amounts of time watching online videos of the little polar bear drinking out of a baby bottle and playing with a soccer ball. My daughter continued, "Why couldn't the film people just catch the starving bears and send them to a zoo?"

I remember having the exact same thought when I grew up watching reruns of *Mutual of Omaha's Wild Kingdom*. How could Marlin Perkins stand by and let that lion kill that wildebeest? Why didn't he intervene when the cobra went after the mongoose? I turned to my youngest and said the same, ineffectual words my mom had said to me: "They can't, honey. It's nature's way."

Arctic Tale was an engrossing story with incredible footage. The team of filmmakers had spent fifteen years in the Arctic documenting the walrus and polar bear families. And while it was entertaining, there was no missing the message. Global warming is having a terrible impact on the Arctic. The summer sea ice has shrunk by twenty percent in recent decades. The winter ice returns three months later than it used to, and breaks up much earlier. If climate change continues at this rate, the ocean could be virtually ice-free by the summer of 2040!

The effects on the Arctic animals are devastating. Seals no longer have time to build birthing caves in the snow, so their babies are born out in the open, vulnerable to predators (we saw a very close call between a ringed seal pup and a hungry polar bear). Whole families of walruses are stuck on tiny ice rafts, because even walruses will freeze if they stay in the water too long. And polar bears are starving.

The poor bears spend the summer months hunting for seals on the sea ice, preparing for eight long months of hibernation. But with the sea ice melting, they're not able to find enough food to sustain them, and are now threatened with extinction. The bears wake hungry and must desperately find food before they starve to death.

The kids and I munched our popcorn as we watched the mother polar bear and her two cubs roam the shrinking ice in their hopeless search for sustenance. As predicted, it did not go well. The little male polar bear was weakening. He was starting to stumble and soon lay down to sleep. His mother and sister cuddled him, trying to keep him warm. Oh shit. He was dying, wasn't he? The kids were going to lose it.

Through my tear-filled eyes, I glanced at my son. Ethan looked a little misty, but he was otherwise fine. Almost fearfully, I looked over at Tegan, president of the polar bear fan club. I expected to see her in a sobbing, shivering puddle of saline, but other than the glint of unshed tears in her eyes, she was holding it together. I, on the other hand, was not. The poor little fella wasn't going to make it. I knew it was coming but that didn't make it any easier. His mom and sister were devastated. Polar bears had feelings! And this wasn't "nature's way." This was our fault. We humans were destroying their habitat with our selfish, polluting ways. It was so sad. So wrong!

At the end of the movie (I had composed myself somewhat by this time), perky child actors came on screen with environmental messages for the viewers.

"Turn off lights when you leave a room!" a girl chirped.

"We already do that," I replied smugly.

"Unplug appliances when you're not using them!" Another kid suggested.

"Already taken care of."

"Be sure to recycle!"

I nodded to my children flanking me. "Of course."

"Use reusable shopping bags!"

"Done."

"Tell your parents to get a hybrid car!"

Obviously, we weren't quite that good.

"Take shorter showers!" Another child cried.

"Yeah, you two," I said, shooting my kids a look. Seriously, Ethan and Tegan had been taking the longest showers in the history of showers. We had installed the one low-flow showerhead, but by somewhere around twenty minutes I don't think it matters anymore. What were they doing in there? They weren't old enough to be doing anything, you know . . . *teenager-ish*. They didn't have superfluous body hair to shave. What was the holdup?

The next time Tegan (world-record holder for long showers) was in the shower, I had some new ammunition. While she'd previously ignored my entreaties to hurry up, after watching *Arctic Tale*, she could no longer ignore the dilemma of the polar bear.

"Time to get out," I called into the bathroom. "You're killing a baby polar bear."

The water turned off. It was like magic!

So I already knew that my kids had concerns about global warming, but I wondered how it was affecting other children. My offspring were genetically predisposed to be worrywarts. Maybe not all kids were so distressed by the doom-and-gloom information overload? I decided it couldn't hurt to ask some of the neighborhood children for their thoughts on the environment.

I was driving Ethan and two of his ten-year-old classmates on a field trip to the Richmond Nature Park when I decided to broach the subject. As the three boys in the backseat chattered excitedly about soccer and video games, I interjected.

"Hey, David and Ryan," I said, "Could I ask you a question?"

"Sure," they replied gamely.

"Do you worry about global warming?"

There was an instant pall on the backseat hilarity. Finally, Ryan said softly, "Yes."

I hadn't anticipated that my question would have such a sobering effect. But I decided to continue. Since I'd already knocked the wind out of their sails, I may as well. "Do you know a lot about global warming?"

"Just that it's really bad," Ryan replied, his voice breaking a little.

David added morosely, "Pollution is causing problems with the ozone layer and the earth is heating up."

"That's right," I said, keeping my tone cheerful. "So where do you learn about the environment?"

"Our teacher tells us about it sometimes," one of them mumbled.

"And TV."

"Great! Thanks guys." This was followed by a long, dreary silence. I hadn't meant to upset them, but global warming was obviously a major downer. I had ruined their field trip before we even got there. What if we showed up at the Richmond Nature Park and they were in tears? They'd tell their teacher and he would ban me from field-trip driving forevermore. This would be a blessing in a way, but it could reflect poorly on Ethan. I had to do something.

"So guys . . . what's your favorite type of sports car?" Luckily, this tried-and-true topic change worked, and the kids returned to their former vigor.

It was now apparent that my kids were not the only ones who worried about climate change. If Ryan and David were any indication, it was weighing heavily on the minds of our youth. One Saturday morning, I was helping a friend prepare for a fund-raiser. As I was washing dozens of coffee cups, her nine-year-old son walked into the kitchen.

"Hey, Mark," I said brightly, "do you worry about global warming?"

"Not really," he replied flippantly, "until I watch a documentary about it. And then I wish I wasn't alive right now."

My stomach lurched. He wished he wasn't alive when he thought about global warming? I should never have brought it up. When would I learn?

He continued. "I wish I lived millions of years ago so I could have made some changes."

Okay, it wasn't a death wish, but still . . . That was the last time I asked someone else's child about their fears regarding climate change. I didn't want to become known as the "Global Warming Mom." And I didn't want Ethan's friends to desert him. When he'd ask them to come over, they'd say, "No thanks. Your mom makes me feel depressed."

I couldn't turn to Tegan's friends. They were little girls! They'd probably start bawling. When they went to bed, they'd have nightmares. Their parents would rush to comfort them. "What's wrong, honey?"

"Tegan's mom made me talk about how we'll all be cooked to death!"

The next day, I'd probably get a phone call. "We'd like you to pay for Marissa's therapy sessions."

Instead, I decided to let the parents do the dirty work for me. Questions about global warming weren't nearly as depressing when they came from your own loving mom or dad. I sent a mass e-mail out to a bunch of my friends who have kids. It was a simple questionnaire.

> Do you talk to your kids about global warming?
>
> Do they worry about it?
>
> Do they know information about it that you have not told them? Where did they hear it?
>
> Do they try to be environmentally friendly?

The message went to about fifteen parents. One friend forwarded it on to her soccer teams (both indoor and outdoor) and parents of her sons' hockey teammates. Now that it had been circulated to about sixty parents, I could just sit back and wait.

I waited. And I waited. Eventually, I got three responses—three. Out of sixty! I knew that a lot of parents were busy juggling work and children and volunteering and Christmas shopping (the timing may have been bad). But only three? Of course, it was entirely possible that they just didn't want to sit their kids down and say, "Hey sweetie, let's talk about the end of the world."

But the three responses I got were excellent. My friend Ted told me a great story about how he went to kiss his son good night and found him crying inconsolably.

"What's wrong?" Ted asked gently.

"I'm worried about global warming," the six-year-old wailed.

"Oh son, don't worry about it," Ted soothed. "It'll be okay."

"Easy for you to say," the boy snapped. "You'll be *dead!*"

Another friend, Leslie, told me her children knew lots of ways to stop global warming: don't drive your car too much, turn off the lights, bring cloth bags to the grocery store, don't smoke, don't smoke pot...

"Absolutely," Leslie replied, "All of those are excellent ways to save the environment."

My friend Corina informed me via e-mail that her son, Shae, was quite knowledgeable on the subject. His class had been watching the *Planet Earth* series at school, and he'd been learning about endangered species in the rain forest and the Arctic.

"Shae said that polar bears are being forced down south and mating with grizzly bears," she wrote to me.

I chuckled when I read it. It was so cute how kids got things mixed up. It reminded me of when Ethan told me that in seventeen years, the entire continent of Australia would be covered in garbage.

"Where did you hear that?" I asked.

"When we were living in Australia. They said it would happen in twenty years, but that was three years ago."

Obviously, the entire continent of Australia wasn't going to be covered in garbage. And obviously a polar bear couldn't mate with a grizzly bear. That was like a chimpanzee mating with a giraffe. Or a raccoon and a pheasant. Okay, maybe it wasn't *that* bizarre. It was more like a lion mating with a tiger . . . to produce a liger. Or a horse and a donkey creating a mule. But those were captive animals whose pairing was orchestrated by humans. Would a polar bear really *choose* to do it with a grizzly bear? Polar bears are so beautiful and majestic and grizzly bears have that big hump on their back and such matted fur. And a grizzly bear is an aggressive animal. Wouldn't it just want to kill the polar bear on sight? I just couldn't believe it.

So I googled it: Polar bear mating with grizzly bear.

Shae was right. It was real. Oh my god! In 2006, hunters in the Canadian Arctic had shot this weird-looking bear that had white fur with brown patches and long claws. The poor bear had also inherited the unfortunate grizzly hump. DNA proved it was a hybrid.

It's no wonder kids are freaked-out! I don't mean to sound like some kind of bear racist, but what kind of crazy world are we living in? What's next? As the ice caps melt, will penguins head south to get it on with seagulls? Will we see puffins mating with robins? Reindeers having sex with cows? Okay, I'm going off on a tangent here, but you see what I'm saying.

So how do we talk to our kids about the sad state of the world today? Apparently, we have to do it very gently. My neighbor George is a university professor specializing in sustainable communities. He was part of a u.s. national committee brought together by the Unilever Foundation (yes, Unilever Ponds has an interest in the environment and education) whose goal was to propose a new model for environmental education for children, from kindergarten through grade seven.

By talking to children in this age group, the committee discovered something surprising. The more that kids knew about the precarious state of the environment, the fewer positive actions they took. The kids couldn't process information about melting ice caps, devastating storms, and dead polar bears. They ended up feeling overwhelmed and helpless, paralyzed by fear and dread. As a result, they just threw up their hands and said, "What's the point of recycling? The world's going to end anyway."

The committee recommended that children not be told that the planet is in dire straits. Instead, it's best to focus on kids' small world. They proposed teaching kids where the water goes when it goes down the drain, why it's okay that a leaf turns brown and crumbles into the dirt, how trees give us the air we breathe, and how, without bees, nothing would grow. They suggested that younger children map the ecological workings of their own two blocks and, as they got older, add more space and distance. Basically, the committee concluded that it is best to foster a love and understanding of nature and the earth so that children will grow up wanting to protect it.

It made so much sense—for the kids, and for me! There was no point focusing on the things I couldn't control or change. I would simply concentrate on my own backyard, my own community. It was futile to worry about the fact that the United States pumped about seven thousand megatons of greenhouse gases into the atmosphere in 2004 (according to *The Hot Topic*). And why obsess about China, which is said to have recently overtaken the United States for the title of world's biggest polluter (though China only produces about five tons of carbon per capita, whereas the United States and Canada each emit about twenty-four tons per person).

I decided then and there not to feel depressed and defeated about the earth's future. I wouldn't obsess about what governments were doing (or not doing). Instead, I would focus on my own small world and make sure it was as green as it could be . . . Okay, as green as I was willing to make it. And by so doing, I'd set a good example for my children and make them feel that their parents' generation cared about their future . . . and their children's future . . . and their children's children's future.

My British friend Kirsten was doing a good job. She was even interviewed on the radio because she was worm composting with her thirteen-year-old son. I decided to ask her how her positive steps had affected him.

"He feels quite optimistic about the future of the planet," she said. "He sees people taking action and it makes him feel like we're going to be okay."

"That's great."

"Of course, he's wrong," she said. "Throwing a handful of potato peelings to a bunch of worms once a week isn't going to stop climate change. It needs to happen at a governmental level."

"No, no," I said. "Don't think that way. Focus on your own small world and feel good about the green steps you're taking. I mean, you're worm composting. That's so great!"

"It's a nightmare!" she cried. "I'm not sure how much longer I can bear it. The worms are these horrible, red, wriggling things. Every time I open the lid, I'm terrified they're going to jump out and crawl all over me."

Despite her worm-induced terror, Kirsten's worm composting *was* making a difference. It wouldn't stop global warming in its tracks, but it was making her son feel better about the future, and that was important, too. And all those little green things I was doing were reassuring my kids.

So I guess we're lucky, in a way, when our children come to us with their fears about climate change. Our parents could only say: "I'm *fairly certain* there won't be a nuclear war" or "you *probably* won't get a brain tumor." Oh, how reassuring! At least we can take positive action to allay our kids' concerns. And maybe it's working. With all the green stuff we've been doing, the kids really believe we can save the polar bears—and the planet. In fact, it's been months since either of them has asked me: Will our house be under water when the ice caps melt, or will we just be living at the beach?

My Small
Green World

IT WAS A revelation. I wasn't going to obsess about the big, gloomy environmental picture. I was going to focus on my own little world—which basically consisted of my house, the grocery store, and my kids' school. (Kind of pathetic, but true.) Our home was already quite green. And I was trying to make sustainable food choices when I did the grocery shopping. But how did Bayview Community School measure up?

I'd always thought our school was pretty good. I mean, a school in the heart of Kitsilano had to have an environmental conscience. And Bayview certainly did. It promoted "Walk to School Week" (which we did daily), and some classes had made their own worm composters. Most teachers encouraged students to use both sides of paper, and older kids were asked to hand in typed assignments on computer memory sticks. Tegan's second-grade class used all-organic ingredients on baking day, and her teacher had set up a blog in place of a class newsletter in order to save paper. My son's class, being a little older, often walked or took public transit on their field trips. The teachers and administrators at Bayview were definitely making an effort.

It was probably two years earlier when Ethan had brought a note home from school.

"We're supposed to pack litterless lunches," he said, handing me the slip of paper.

"Your lunches barely have any litter," I said, feeling quite satisfied with my lunch-packing program.

"Yeah, but we're supposed to have *no* litter," he replied, walking casually to his room. I perused the note and found that Ethan was right. The letter said that on average, one child with a disposable lunch generates 67 pounds of waste over the course of the school year. That meant that an average-sized elementary school, with 300 students, produced 20,100 pounds of lunchtime garbage.

I immediately thought of my own school years: 67 pounds of waste times 7 years in elementary school equaled 469 pounds of garbage. Add to that my two brothers' lunches, and my immediate family alone had contributed over fourteen hundred pounds of wax paper to the Quesnel, BC, town dump. And that was just elementary school. It's not like I got better once I reached high school. Every day for lunch I bought a bag of nacho-cheese chips and a chocolate bar from the vending machine. (I still can't believe I did that—and didn't weigh four hundred pounds.) I had a lot to atone for.

I was going to do it! I was going litterless. How hard could it be? The newsletter suggested checking out the Web site www.laptoplunches.com for waste-free lunch ideas. The site also sells reusable plastic bento boxes, thermoses, and various other containers, but I went the cheap and easy route. I headed down to the nearby dollar store and bought reusable lunch bags (only a dollar each), two sandwich boxes, and four small, plastic containers. I picked up a few stainless steel spoons, too (I didn't want the kids losing the ones from my matching set). I was ready. I just had to go to the grocery store.

Suddenly, so many items were off-limits. All those convenient, grab-and-go snacks were big no-no's: individual yogurts, puddings, or applesauces; mini-packs of crackers and cookies. Even granola bars, yogurt tubes, and cheese strings have packaging. The individually wrapped lunch item is a multi-million-dollar industry. I was going to have to make some different choices.

It wasn't so bad. I bought all the same stuff, only in a larger size. Then I conscientiously transferred the items to the various containers. I was a really great litterless-lunch mom! That was, until I tried to send the kids to school with leftover pizza. The triangular slices could not be squeezed into the square sandwich containers. I tried to remain calm, but how the hell was I going to get this pizza to school without creating any waste? I ended up cutting the wedges into tiny, bite-sized pizza morsels. I thought I should alert the kids.

"Today, you're having pizza bites for lunch," I told them, like I'd invented some cool new lunch food.

"Sure," they replied indifferently.

It was great that the kids didn't care what form their lunch arrived in.

And then I baked some muffins. I don't bake muffins very often; in fact, I bake them about once a year. So I was feeling very June Cleaver as I packed the home-baked delights into my children's lunch boxes. But the muffins didn't fit! And when I tried to mash them into the plastic boxes, they crumbled. Pizza bites were one thing; muffin crumbs were quite another. But there was no way I was going to let a sandwich container ruin my kids' special annual lunchtime treat. I was going to have to do it. I was going to have to break down and use a plastic sandwich baggie.

"Please bring this plastic baggie home," I instructed the children. "If anyone sees you with it, tell them we're going to wash it and reuse it at least three or four times."

They looked at me like I was a going a little nutso, but they didn't know the pressure I was under. I couldn't be the lone parent not following the school's litterless-lunch lead!

I'd been making the extra lunch-packing effort for several months when I volunteered for one of Tegan's field trips. We went ice skating, and after an hour or so the kids took a snack break. As the children unpacked their food, I tried to contain my shock. Out came the paper lunch bags full of plastic-wrapped muffins, snack-sized bags of crackers, and plastic tubs of rice pudding complete with disposable spoons. There were granola bars, individual crackers-and-cheese packs, and foil packages of fruit chewies. How could so many parents ignore the litterless-lunch initiative? It was disgraceful. I managed to hide my chagrin from Tegan's classmates. After all, it wasn't their fault that their parents didn't care about the future of the planet.

I looked at certain mothers differently after that, I'll admit. Sure, Taylor's mom, was a very friendly woman who was raising two smart, kind, and well-mannered children. And yes, she was an oncologist at BC Children's Hospital, who had donated her services to aid sick children in war-torn countries. But she had sent her son to school with a mini foil-pack of crackers! It was impossible to forget that.

In a way, this took the pressure off. I no longer had to be wracked with guilt whenever I resorted to using a sandwich baggie. I mean, Bronwyn's parents were sending her to school with Lunchables, for god's sake! But I couldn't go back. I had made a decision to be a litterless-lunch mom, and I was sticking to it. And I actually found that it was cheaper to go the reusable route. For one thing, in Canada we pay GST on individual servings of yogurt and juice boxes, but not on a large container of yogurt or a carton of juice. Manufacturers also charge a premium for the convenience factor.

A chart on wastefreelunches.org broke down the savings. It compared the cost of prepackaged individual servings of popular lunch foods such as yogurt, granola bars, and mini-carrots with regular, larger serving sizes. Without even factoring in the taxes, the individual servings were a lot more expensive. When you threw in a paper napkin and a couple of plastic sandwich bags, they calculated the cost of a disposable lunch at a $1.37 more than a waste-free option.

I mentioned this significant savings to a mom-friend of mine, but she was unimpressed.

"That's a small price to pay for the convenience," she said. "Packing lunches is such a chore already. I'm not going to make it even harder for myself by transferring bulk food into a bunch of little containers."

"But you'd be saving $6.85 a week!" I wanted to say. "Over the course of the average school year, that's about three hundred bucks—per kid! And you have two kids, so you'd save over seven thousand dollars over their twelve years of schooling. That's enough to send them to college! Well . . . for a month or two."

Unfortunately, I'm not good at doing math in my head, so I couldn't actually say any of this. Instead, I told her that saving money wasn't my real reason for doing this. "I'm making environmentally friendly changes in my own small world so that my kids don't get depressed and I don't get a green-guilt-induced stomach ulcer."

She just looked at me. Green guilt obviously wasn't a problem for her.

I'd always sent my kids to school with a reusable water bottle. Even when they were toddlers, I'd packed them off to daycare with a plastic drink container. It was important to stay hydrated. And everyone knew that drinking plain old tap water out of a water fountain was going to kill you. There could be lead in your pipes. There could be manure in your water supply. Someone with the Ebola virus could have stuck their mouth on the spout! To ensure the cleanest water possible for my kids, I used a filter to remove heavy metals and pesticide residues. Then I sent them off with a plastic bottle full of clean, filtered water. Wasn't I a good mother?

I thought I was, until I watched the news one night. "Mountain Equipment Co-op is removing plastic water bottles from their shelves because they will KILL YOU!" the anchorman said (or something similarly foreboding). I continued to watch for more details. These polycarbonate bottles contained bisphenol A, which mimics estrogen and is derived from petrochemicals. Bisphenol A had been linked, in dozens of independent research studies, to illnesses that might be caused by hormone disruption. The news report said that the bottles in question were made by Nalgene and had a recycling symbol "7" on the bottom. I hurried to check my kids' drink containers. Tegan's was a Rubbermaid bottle so was fine, but Ethan's was Nalgene. I flipped it over and found the number "7."

Oh god! I was poisoning my son with toxic fake estrogen. Now he was going to get man boobs from his water bottle. Or something much worse—like a tumor on his salivary glands! Christ! I couldn't win. I threw both water bottles into the recycling bin. Tegan's wasn't made of the controversial polycarbonate, but suddenly any plastic just seemed too risky. I went to a drugstore and bought two aluminum water bottles. I suppose any day now I'll hear that people are getting aluminum poisoning from their water containers, but so far, so good.

The plastic scare had gotten me thinking about . . . well, how scary plastic is. It's a miraculous invention, but every single

piece of plastic that was ever produced still exists. It takes millions of years for plastic to biodegrade, and it can leach toxic
chemicals into the earth, our food, and our water.

I had read an article in the December 2007 issue of *Esquire*
magazine about a new kind of plastic. A chemist has invented
a way to make plastic out of a chemical compound made from
orange peels called limonene, which he mixes with carbon
dioxide and a catalyst. He can make everything from plastic
wrap to bottles to electronics containers (for TVs, stereos, DVD
players, etc.). And the plastic will naturally biodegrade in just a
few months. It can actually be produced using recycled carbon
dioxide from carbon-belching factories, so even *making* it is
good for the environment. According to the article, it will be
used in high-end electronics within a couple of years, and food
containers will follow soon after. I can't wait! You can't feel bad
about filling your kids' water bottle when the plastic is made
from orange peels.

So maybe not all parents were as good as I was about litterless lunches, but I still felt quite positive about the greenness
of my neighborhood school. Not only was Bayview doing a
fairly decent job of being environmentally friendly (I say *fairly
decent* because the Vancouver School Board still doesn't have
a district-wide recycling program in place) but they were teaching the kids to care about the earth and all its creatures. When
Ethan was in third grade, he came rushing home from school
insisting that we make a donation to save the spirit bear.

"The what?" I asked him.

"The spirit bear."

"Is it a real bear? Because I'm not going to donate money to save some myth or legend or something."

"Yeah, it's a real bear," he retorted, like he couldn't believe he'd been birthed by such an idiot. "They're also known as a Kermode bear. They're a white bear but they're not a polar bear. They're a subspecies of the black bear and they only live on the coast of BC."

"Oh right," I said, pretending I had heard of spirit bears before. Why hadn't I heard of spirit bears before?

"They're Canada's rarest bear and they don't live anywhere else in the world. The native people believe they're magical. But they're in danger now because their habitat is being destroyed for logging. We've got to do something."

"Of course," I said, though I was not going to do anything that involved camping out in a forest where bears lived . . . or even in a forest where no bears lived, for that matter.

"We can donate to the Valhalla Wilderness Society," Ethan told me. "They're working to save the spirit bears' habitat."

It sure beat camping. So I got out my checkbook and we made a donation to save the spirit bear. I can't remember how much it was—maybe fifty, maybe only twenty dollars, but it gave Ethan peace of mind. We received a thank-you note from the Valhalla Wilderness Society and continue to receive updates on the plight of the spirit bear.

About a year later, Ethan had moved on to another cause. The students in his science class had been assigned a report on an endangered species. Ethan chose the Bengal tiger and was alarmed by what he discovered.

"Did you know that in the last fifty years, three types of tigers have become extinct?" he told me. "The Bali, Caspian, and Javan."

"Oh my god!"

"There are less than forty-five hundred Bengal tigers left in the wild. There are only about fifty South China tigers, less than five hundred Siberian and Sumatran tigers, and fewer than two thousand Indochinese tigers."

"Yikes!"

"There are more captive tigers in the United States than there are wild tigers left in the whole world. We have to do something!"

He was right, we did. But as I was about to head for my checkbook, something stopped me. Maybe having his mom write a check every time he wanted to save an animal from extinction wasn't really sending Ethan the right message. Maybe it was giving him the erroneous impression that his mom actually had a lot of money that she could throw at any cause that struck his fancy. Maybe it would be better to have him learn about donating his own money to worthy causes?

"I have an idea," I said. "How much money do you have saved up?"

"About fifteen dollars," he said, already looking nervous.

"If you donate your fifteen dollars to save the tigers, I'll match your donation. That way, we'll be donating thirty dollars."

He looked at me liked I'd suggested he donate his corneas to Project Tiger. "Umm . . . I was actually saving up for this cool toy space station."

"I thought you wanted to save the tigers?" I remarked. "Isn't that more important than a plastic space station?"

Then I saw the conflict on his sweet little ten-year-old face. Space station versus tiger extinction . . . it was a tough decision for a guy his age. "Don't worry," I said, "you don't have to use your own money." His immense relief was evident. He wrapped me in a huge hug.

So maybe I didn't have the heart to teach Ethan about the financial realities of his kind and caring nature. But I loved that he had such a strong social conscience. And he really believed that he could make a difference. That's probably why he joined the Bayview Spirit Team. The Spirit Team, in case it's not obvious, was about school spirit. They initiated fun theme days like "crazy hair day" and "wear your pajamas to school day." They also spearheaded several charity drives. And they had an environmental focus, as well.

Being the doting mother that I am, I asked Ethan for some specifics about his involvement in the team. He was a little vague.

"We get together at lunch and we have meetings and we're in teams," he said.

"And what do the teams do?"

"Some people make 'Don't smoke' signs and put them up all over the school."

"That's good," I responded. "What did your team do?"

"Well, we were going to wear green T-shirts and burst into people's classes and say 'Bayview Green Team!'"

"So you'd make sure kids were good to the environment?"

"Yeah, like recycling and not buying Hummers and stuff," he explained. "But then it didn't work out."

I had to ask, "Why not?"

"Because we wanted to use these green T-shirts that another class used for the school play, and we wanted to get them printed with 'Bayview Green Team.'" But then we couldn't get the T-shirts and it wouldn't work without the T-shirts."

It was a shame. I wondered how many Hummers were unwittingly bought because the Bayview Green Team couldn't get their shirts printed.

A few months later, the school newsletter mentioned that another Spirit Team initiative was raising a bunch of chum fry (baby salmon for all you landlubbers) in a large tank in the front hallway. When the fry were old enough, the team released them into a creek leading to the ocean.

"That's so cool," I said to my son. "Why didn't you tell me about it?

"Well . . ." Ethan replied, "I actually happened to see one of the chum fry having a seizure." (He imitated the chum fry seizure.) "It died. And two other chum fry also broke their fins, and they died too. I don't want to talk about it."

I guess it was kind of traumatic. Still, I thought it was a great lesson on the fragility of salmon.

Tegan was also learning about nature at school. Her class had been selected to participate in a "Scientist in Residence" program over a three-month period. The scientist, a British woman in her sixties named Dr. Higgins, would spend time in the classroom teaching the children about the forest through hands-on experiments and lessons.

My youngest has always been an enthusiastic learner, and the sessions with Dr. Higgins proved very exciting for her. Tegan would come home from school full of scintillating information.

"Do you know how to tell if a tree is a hemlock, a pine, a Douglas-fir, or a cedar?" she asked me.

"No," I said, a tad embarrassed. I'd grown up in a town supported by the forest industry, after all. Shouldn't I know that? But then, given that the forest industry meant chopping down the hemlocks, pines, Douglas firs, and cedars, maybe it was better not to get too attached.

"A hemlock's needles are all different sizes. A Douglas-fir's are all the same size. A pine tree's are long and spiky, and a cedar's has scales."

"Thanks," I said, trying to take it all in. I was a little long in the tooth to be learning this for the first time, but better late than never.

A week or so later, Tegan came home from school with an announcement. "We're going on a nature walk through the forest with Dr. Higgins!" she said. "Can you come?"

What better way to foster my daughter's love of nature than this? And who knew what kind of helpful nature hints I could learn from Dr. Higgins? "Of course I'll volunteer," I said.

It was a beautiful day as Dr. Higgins led us through the trails in Pacific Spirit Regional Park. The children eagerly identified the different types of trees and pointed out nurse logs and various fungi. We used loupes to examine moss and flowers and different species of insects inhabiting the forest floor. Dr. Higgins peppered the children with questions as we travelled.

"What are the vessels that take water up inside the tree?" she asked.

"Xylem!" one of Tegan's classmates called out.

"And what are the vessels that take food down inside the tree?"

Several hands shot up. Tegan was selected to answer.

"The phloem," my daughter said. The kid was a frickin' genius!"

I left the forest that day a little calmer, a little wiser, and a little more optimistic. At Bayview Community School, both my children were learning to appreciate nature and all its creatures. And at home, I was doing my part to raise responsible citizens of the planet. This focusing-on-our-own-small-world thing was really working for us.

And then things changed. I was waiting outside to escort my children home after school one day when they both emerged carrying large white envelopes. Both kids handed me their packages and promptly ran off to play. I opened one of them to find a catalog for wrapping paper and various other unnecessary gift items. It was fund-raising time again.

When Ethan started school in Calgary, we didn't have to fund-raise. At the beginning of the year, parents were asked to make a contribution (I think it was forty dollars per child) in lieu of participating in fund-raising projects. For some families this was a bit steep, so they were given the option of paying in instalments or opting out all together. I don't think this had much to do with the environment. It was probably because everyone in Calgary is rich and too busy renovating their house to fund-raise. Regardless, I was happy to make the donation. We were new to the city and had no relatives in the area. Who was going to buy our fund-raising crap?

Our Australian school had been a different story. One day as I dropped Tegan off at "kindie," Mrs. Lake said, "Don't forget your box of chocolate-covered malt balls."

"A box of malt balls? For me?" I thought. "Is this because I volunteered to help them make fruit salad the other day? What a nice gesture." But what Mrs. Lake meant was a crate of chocolate-covered malt balls for me to sell. When I went to pick up Ethan, I was similarly given a crate of individually wrapped chocolate frogs. On each box was a note: "PLEASE DO NOT RETURN UNSOLD PRODUCT."

I almost cried. What was I supposed to do with fifty chocolate treats? I knew no one in Perth except my in-laws and other school parents who had their own candies to sell. I hit up my mother-in-law. Yes, she had nine other fund-raising grandchildren, but surely she'd help me out here.

"I don't really like malt balls or chocolate frogs," she said.

"Who cares!" I wanted to cry. "Buy some and throw them out!" But I was the woman who had stolen her youngest son from her and moved him to the other side of the world. I knew I couldn't guilt-trip her about school chocolates.

Instead, I bought both crates and ate the frickin' things myself. Seriously, I ate twenty-five boxes of malt balls (I fed most of the frogs to the kids). And I threw out twenty-five cardboard packages and twenty-five plastic frog-wrappers. And at three bucks a treat, it cost me a lot more than forty bucks per kid.

So here I was, at my fairly green school in my very green neighborhood, and I was being asked to sell wrapping paper. Wrapping paper? That didn't seem very environmentally friendly. One of the Bayview moms took a stand and refused to sell it. "I'm against wrapping paper," she said. "It's wasteful and unnecessary and kills too many trees."

But anyone with kids in school knows that the whole experience is a little like being back in school yourself. You want to fit in. You want to be liked! And I wasn't really "against" wrapping paper. I just thought it should be used sparingly. I ended up buying six rolls and a can of chocolate-covered popcorn.

The following year we sold coupon books: approximately four hundred pages of coupons redeemable for goods and services. Not great for the environment, but probably slightly better than wrapping paper. But as an incentive, kids were invited to sign up on a Web site to win all sorts of junk: holographic sunglasses, puzzle-cube erasers, and expanding dinosaurs in eggs. Why were we encouraging consumption of this garbage? And why were we turning our young children into mini-capitalists by rewarding the ones who sold the most stuff? (Okay, I'm really sounding like a pinko hippy now.)

I brought the idea of cash in lieu of fundraising up with a parent council member, who felt it would be a hardship for many of our families. I totally understood. I wasn't exactly frolicking naked on a bed covered in hundred-dollar bills every night. But wasn't selling stuff to people who didn't want it a hardship, too? I always felt too sheepish to flog stuff to anyone who wasn't a close relative. And even then, I was a little hesitant.

But with the coupon books, I thought I would at least try to broaden my scope. There were some good coupons in there for some great restaurants. I sent an e-mail to a select few friends who I thought just might be interested in buying one. No one responded but my friend Trevor. "You've changed," he wrote. "The Robyn I know would never send an e-mail like this." So as always, I bought a coupon book myself and sold one to my mom.

I suppose it's possible that some people enjoy taking their kids' fund-raising chocolates into the office and selling them to their coworkers. Perhaps they're entirely comfortable conning their grandma into purchasing eight rolls of wrapping paper or a coupon book she'll never use. And maybe part of my desire to hand over a check instead is just plain laziness? In fact, I'm sure that a big part of it is. That's why I sit back and make comments but never actually join the parent council and help implement my ideas. (I'm just not a committee type of person.)

Recently, I spoke with our parent council president, who told me they were moving toward direct donation. She plans to set up a school Web site with links: "support our computer lab" or "support our new playground." This will allow parents, or any philanthropist, to go online and make an anonymous contribution. And I, for one, will absolutely be donating. There will still be fund-raising initiatives, I'm sure, but hopefully no more wrapping paper . . . Although that chocolate-covered popcorn was really good.

14

Happy
Sustainable
Birthday

• • •

SURE, I CAN feel good that I am fostering a love of nature and environmental responsibility in my children. Yes, I think their education is helping them understand that the earth is in a precarious situation, but that all is not lost. And I really believe I'm taking positive, green steps to set a good example for my kids and allay their fears about the future of the planet. And then their birthdays roll around.

The problem I have with birthday parties is the stuff. Jane Goodall once said in an interview that *stuff* will be the end of civilization. Try telling that to a ten-year-old with a room full of construction blocks or a seven-year-old buried in plastic fashion dolls. My mom says I'm a minimalist, but I don't think I'd go that far. I just don't like to have a lot of crap lying around that I don't need—which makes me a minimalist, I guess. Somehow, despite their genetics, both my kids are total pack-rats. It's ridiculous and a little disturbing. They will hold on to the smallest, most inconsequential piece of plastic garbage for years.

I walked into Tegan's room one day and just about had a heart attack. The buildup of crapola was downright terrifying! I had to intervene. If I didn't do something soon, my daughter would be buried by an avalanche of plastic bouncy balls, Halloween spider rings, little purses, and erasers.

"We've got to get rid of some of this stuff," I announced.

"What?" My daughter shrieked. "Why?"

"Because," I grumbled, approaching a display of five different lip glosses, six poppies left over from Remembrance Day, and nine notepads in various shapes, laid out on a little table in her room. "It's junk. You don't need it."

Her eyes filled with tears and her voice trembled as she said, "But these are my *collections*."

"Collections?" I scoffed, as I took in the groupings of pencil cases, a cluster of half-empty tubes of hand lotion, and several stress balls. "This is all just..." The despair on my daughter's face stopped me from saying "crap." I didn't have the heart to tell her she was basically collecting garbage like some crazy old bag lady. "Okay," I gave in. "If you're *collecting* all this stuff, I guess it can stay."

I moved on to my son's room. Surely it couldn't be as bad as his sister's. But it was! On his dresser alone I found a fake nose, two sets of fake teeth (one was vampire fangs, one was a "grill"), and fake bling. There was also a grip-strengthener, a gold pig, a puppet he made when he was five, a Hacky Sack, and a small plastic Buddha.

"Honey," I said, as gently as I could, "I think we need to get rid of some of this junk."

"Junk?" he said, incredulous. "There's no junk here."

"Ummm . . ." I waved my hand around to indicate the pile of hockey pucks, the squirt guns, the round John Lennon glasses, and a ceramic echidna.

"I need all this stuff," he said bluntly.

"What about these rocks?" I said, lifting one of five large, plastic buckets filled with rocks he and his uncle have collected over the years. "Surely we can get rid of some of these?"

Ethan just looked at me. "Mom . . . I'm really into rocks, remember?"

Obviously, I was going to have to invade their rooms while they were at school and chuck out all their crap. But it wasn't that simple any more, was it? "Chucking out" was now synonymous with "letting languish in a landfill for thousands of years." It all had to be appropriately donated or recycled.

At least some of the plastic made-in-China junk was recyclable. It was a time-consuming task, searching (often in vain) for a recycling symbol on all those plastic toys and figurines. And what about all those ancient art projects? If I pulled the pipe-cleaner antennae and the plastic googly eyes off that egg-carton caterpillar, it could go into the blue bin. That made me feel a little better, until Tegan got home from school.

"Hey! What's the egg-carton caterpillar that I made doing in the recycling box? Where are its eyes and antennae?"

Getting rid of their stuff was not going to be easy.

Maybe pack-rat-itis skips a generation, because my mom has it too. And she seems determined to cultivate it in her grandchildren. She's always showing up at my house with more stuff for them.

"I went to the hockey game and they gave me these great plastic pom-pom shakers and plastic rings and six of these great fabric banners with tassels that hang off plastic rods."

And:

"I found this old calligraphy set that belonged to one of your brothers. All the ink has dried up and some of the nibs are broken, but I thought Ethan might like to learn calligraphy."

And another time:

"Someone gave me this set of hideously ugly, gold-embroidered makeup and jewelry bags. I thought Tegan should have them."

She tries to fob stuff off on me, too.

"Do you need a set of casserole dishes with no lids?"

"No thanks."

"Are you sure? Because last time I was at your house, you didn't have many casserole dishes."

"Yeah, that's because I don't need many casserole dishes, especially ones with no lids."

And on another occasion:

"Do you need another set of dishes?"

"No thank you."

"Cutlery?"

"We're good."

"Well," she said, "you definitely do need these cut-glass dessert dishes."

"Okay," I gave in. And I actually do use the dessert dishes quite frequently. I guess my mom is doing a good thing by passing on her used items. But then I am the one stuck finding space for them because I feel too bad about chucking them out.

I sometimes worry that my kids are going to grow up to be hoarders. I saw an Oprah show on it once. It's a real psychological condition where you just keep buying stuff and buying stuff and you are actually incapable of throwing it out. (The actress Delta Burke once mentioned in an interview that she has the affliction.) Eventually, the hoarder ends up living in a house full of old clothes and stacks of magazines, and a family of raccoons has made a nest in the kitchen and she can't even find it. On Oprah, they sent in this expert "de-clutterer" to help a hoarding woman get her house back in order. When they threw out some of her old dress patterns, she screamed like they were ripping her skin off!

I've always tried to curb my children's materialistic dispositions. Ethan, perhaps even more than his sister, has a very strong acquisitive streak. In fact, he can be downright greedy. He's a Taurus, you see. While I don't necessarily believe that all astrological profiling is true, I know three Tauruses who have a shopping addiction. I happened to mention this trait to Ethan, who decided it was a viable excuse for his constant desire for more and more stuff. Whenever I suggest that he doesn't really need any more toys and ask why he doesn't donate some of the stuff he doesn't play with to charity or hand it down to his cousins, he has a standard response. "I like stuff. I can't help it. It's my materialistic Taurus nature."

When I was a kid, we sponsored a child in Haiti through Foster Parents Plan (now called Plan Canada). I loved corresponding with Maria and exchanging photographs. And our relationship taught me a valuable lesson about how children lived in other parts of the world. So when Ethan was about two, we sponsored a little girl in Zambia named Esther. Obviously, I wanted to help Esther and her community, but I also wanted to teach my children about charity and the existence of poverty. A few years ago, we sponsored another girl, named Fatuma, in Tanzania.

The kids have been great about corresponding with their "foster sisters," as they call them. They send them pictures they've drawn and photos of our family. We buy the girls small gifts, like hair ribbons and sticker books. It takes months and months for these presents to make their way to the remote villages. And after months and months, we sometimes get a letter or photos back.

Esther once sent us a picture she had drawn of a cow, some beans, and a cup. (I'm assuming she was instructed to draw some ways that Plan Canada had helped her community, as these seem an odd choice of subject matter.) She was quite a talented artist, but she had drawn all the items using a pink pencil crayon.

Tegan looked at it. "That's such a nice picture," she said. "But I wonder how come she used pink for everything?"

"Because," I explained, "Esther probably only has that one pink pencil crayon. Not everyone in the world has 420 pencil crayons with 8 different shades of pink like we do."

My daughter looked perplexed for a moment then she slowly nodded her head with comprehension.

If Esther only knew how much mileage I've gotten out of that pink crayon. Whenever my kids yearned for some toy they saw on TV, I'd say, "Do you really think you need it? Remember, Esther only has one pink pencil crayon." Or when they complained that a friend had more cool stuff than they did, I'd say, "Yeah? Well Esther only has one pink crayon. How'd you like to be her?" It got to the point where I could just hold up my finger and say "one pink pencil crayon" and save the whole lecture.

So given my great efforts to turn my children into minimalists, is it any wonder that their birthdays fill me with dread? Part of that dread stems from the stress of having to spend two hours with six to ten sugar-filled children who have somehow forgotten all their manners and gone completely deaf to my pleas to settle down. The other part of the dread comes from all those presents. My kids did not need six to ten more little plastic toys to add to their hoarders' paradises.

I had heard that one of the moms at school had done a no-gifts party for her child. She'd asked the birthday guests to bring money instead of presents. Her daughter had donated half the money to a charity of her choice and used the rest to buy something she really wanted. So when Tegan's seventh birthday rolled around, I made my pitch.

"I've got a good idea!" I said. "Why don't you ask your birthday guests to bring ten dollars instead of a gift? You can donate half to charity, and use half to buy something you really want."

Tegan was immediately dismissive. "I think I'm a bit young for that," she said. "Why do you insist on ruining my childhood rights of passage with your minimalist ways?" (Okay, she didn't really say that, but I can practically hear her relaying it to her therapist in about twenty years.)

But by Ethan's tenth birthday in May, I had refined my spiel. "Look," I said, "You've invited eight kids to your party. Do you really want eight little toys that you'll be bored with in a month? Why don't you go for the cash and buy something you really want?"

He quickly did the math. "I'll do it!" he said, rubbing his hands together greedily, his pupils shaped like dollar signs. "I'll do it!"

In keeping with our low-impact-birthday theme, I decided to forego loot bags. I've never understood the concept anyway. Why do children need to be rewarded for spending two hours with their friends playing games and being stuffed with pizza, cake, and pop? We didn't have gift bags when we were young. I'd like to get my hands on the parent who started this whole thing.

I wasn't going to provide loot bags, I decided. I would boycott the plastic parachute men (that make one leap from the top of the stairs and end up hopelessly tangled), the rubber bouncy balls (that always end up behind the couch after they've bounced out of control and knocked a vase off the mantle), and the spider rings (that invoke a panic attack when you stumble upon them in a dusty corner two months later). I knew Tegan liked to add this crap to her "collections" but I was taking a stand. No more glasses with fake noses. No more plastic bracelets and paddleball games and rubber skulls with their eyeballs popping out. No more plastic harmonicas or Pan flutes that made your ears bleed after about twenty minutes of listening to them. Enough!

But at the last minute, I chickened out. What if the kids revolted? Staged some Lord of the Flies–type coup? Or what if poor Ethan was ostracized as "that loser kid who didn't have loot bags?" What if they had a great time at the party, but all they remembered was going home empty-handed? I decided to hand out homemade chocolate chip cookies.

To my surprise, the sustainable birthday party went off without a hitch. Well, there were hitches, but they weren't related to the sustainability. Each kid brought ten dollars, half of which was donated to Ethan's cause du jour, tiger conservation. (It was much easier to donate your own money to save tigers when you still had forty dollars to put toward your space station.) And, thankfully, I was not pummeled with homemade cookies by disgruntled ten-year-olds.

A few months later, Tegan was invited to a birthday party where each child was asked to bring a piece of artwork. The masterpieces would be hung in a birthday-party art gallery. Tegan painted a beautiful picture of pink and purple hearts highlighted with rhinestone stickers. This was her gift for the birthday girl. What a great idea! I loved it.

I loved the idea, but would a seven-year-old? Most of the kids I knew in this age group were of the "give me more" mind-set. How would the birthday girl react to the "art in lieu of toys" concept? When I went to pick Tegan up at the party, I looked at the cute little redhead who had received no dolls or stuffed animals or games for her birthday. She wasn't crying. She wasn't even pouting! She seemed to be having a perfectly good time with her friends and an art gallery full of sad-looking watercolors.

But would Tegan go for it? As we walked home, I thought I might as well ask.

"Would you ever want to have an art-gallery birthday party like Hannah did?"

"Maybe," she said.

"You wouldn't feel disappointed about not getting any presents?"

Ethan jumped in. "I would."

"I know *you* would," I retorted.

Tegan said, "Well, the art is your present."

"That's right," I encouraged her. "And now Hannah can put all those beautiful pictures up on her wall."

"Yeah," Ethan said, "but that's a lame present. Don't do it, Tegan."

"Ethan!" I cried. "If she wants to have an art-gallery party, she should have one. Not everyone's obsessed with getting more and more stuff like you are."

Ethan shrugged. "I'm a materialistic Taurus," he said. "It's my nature."

"I'll think about it," Tegan concluded. "But my next birthday is my *real* birthday, so I don't think I want to have an art-gallery party for that one."

Tegan was right. Her next birthday was only her second *real* birthday. My daughter was born on February 29, a day that only rolls around once every four years. It's not like we ignore the occasion every other year, but when there is an actual February 29 on the calendar, it's a rather big deal. It was a lot to ask an eight-year-old to have an art-gallery party on such a momentous occasion.

As the day approached, Tegan begged to have a Build-A-Bear party. If you're not familiar with Build-A-Bear Workshops, they are a magical place of fun and frolic where kids can select, stuff, and sew up their own teddy bears then buy them really cute and expensive outfits. Build-A-Bear outlets have sprouted up all over the world. Unfortunately (or maybe fortunately), they haven't sprouted up all over Kitsilano. The nearest Build-A-Bear Workshop was about twelve miles away.

When I told one of the green moms about the birthday plans, she suggested I create my own teddy-bear workshop at home. "I can give you some scrap material and you can sew up a few bears."

I looked at her. Sew up a few bears? Who did she think I was, Martha frickin' Stewart? I couldn't sew up a few bears. I could barely sew on a few buttons. No, we were going to have to make the trek out to the Build-A-Bear Workshop in Burnaby. And since our midsize car could only hold three kids, we were going to have to acquire another vehicle. Luckily, my mom volunteered her car and chauffeuring services.

It obviously wasn't very environmentally friendly to drive that far, but Tegan had been dreaming about the Build-A-Bear party for months. And it was only her second *real* birthday. At least, at eight years old, she suddenly felt mature enough to ask for money in lieu of gifts and donated half of it to charity (polar bears, of course). She used the rest to buy a pair of pajamas for Coco, her birthday Build-A-Bear.

To atone for the emissions caused by driving a convoy of eight-year-old-girls out to Burnaby, I have vowed to host low-impact birthday parties from now on. I will eschew paper plates, paper hats, and plastic utensils. I won't give in to the pressure to provide loot bags. And I'll encourage my kids to ask for money instead of gifts and to make a charitable donation with a portion of it. Sure, there will always be some waste associated with birthdays—we can't completely ignore hundreds of years of birthday tradition. But I'm really going to try to throw birthday parties that are kind to the planet . . . and that still provide my kids with some special birthday memories.

Dreaming of a
Green Christmas

• • •

BIRTHDAYS ARE A drop in the environmental bucket compared with Christmas. It really is in a league of its own when it comes to commercialism, consumerism, and waste. I mean, what other holiday has chopping down a tree as its principal tradition? And buying plastic toys powered by toxic batteries then wrapping them in more dead trees as a close second? And how about gorging ourselves on battery-raised turkey and exploitative chocolates?

But two years ago, I decided I would try to do Christmas green. Well . . . green-ish. I knew it wasn't going to be easy. It seems like Christmas is the one time of year we're supposed to forget about the environment or risk being labeled a Scrooge. But given the plethora of "green Christmas" articles that ran in pre-Christmas newspapers and magazines, it could be done.

And I was going to try . . . because I sometimes worry that the holidays aren't quite stressful enough.

I must have read five articles on how to do the festive season up green. From trees to gifts to lights to food, the writers were full of ideas. Unfortunately, a lot of them were not very festive, if not downright pathetic. Was it possible to have a traditional Christmas without harming the planet?

All the articles I read dealt with Christmas trees. I have no idea how many trees have been murdered worldwide in the name of Jesus, but it's got to be quite a few. These are mostly farmed trees that happily give their lives for that very purpose—or so we are led to believe. Since no one has ever communicated with a tree, they might not be the willing sacrificial victims that we think they are. At least you can compost your Christmas tree after the holidays (most cities will pick up your tree and turn it into mulch). But according to the greenies, there were better options.

"Decorate a houseplant instead of a tree," one article suggested. I scoffed. That might work if you lived all by yourself in a small apartment with a couple of cats, but it wasn't going to fly for my family. What would we do on Christmas morning? "Come on kids! Let's gather around the houseplant and open our gifts."

The article also suggested getting a small potted tree that you could water and care for and then, when Christmas was over, plant in your yard. A friend of mine had done this. (It was Valerie Green, of course.)

"We planted it," she said, "but it turned yellow and died." So she went to all the extra effort of loving and nurturing her

Christmas tree, only to be left with a dead yellow tree standing in the front yard? No thanks.

There were organic trees available (according to *Ecoholic*, the vast majority of regular Christmas trees are sprayed with chemicals to keep them looking nice). But organic tree farms were not easy to find. The *Vancouver Sun* recommended a family-run organic tree farm in Mission. Mission? Wasn't driving fifty miles to Mission sort of defeating the purpose?

Well, I already had a plastic tree, anyway. Yes, that's right, plastic. I bought it about ten years ago when I thought I was doing a good thing by not killing a tree every Christmas. I also thought life would be a lot easier if I didn't have to go out and buy a new tree each year, lug it home, and then sweep up its needles for three weeks before I dragged it out to the curb to be mulched. I was right about that part, at least. But I now realize that this Christmas tree will be around a lot longer than I will. Since I don't want to see it in a landfill leaching its plasticky chemicals into the dirt for centuries, I'll have to use it for the rest of my life, and then hand it down to one of my kids. And they'll have to pass it on to their kids, and so on, and so on. As long as there are a few plastic needles clinging to its wire branches, we'll have to keep using it.

The articles I read had a number of suggestions to replace Christmas cards, too: e-cards, text messages, or a link to a Christmas podcast. This would be fine if your Christmas card list was made up of computer-savvy people, but my grandmother is eighty-four. She's probably not going to be able to access that e-card or rock out to that podcast. Another suggestion was to reuse the paper cards you received last year. I'm not kidding.

That was a *real* suggestion! What were you supposed to do—white-out the names and then re-give the card to a loved-one? Yes, I'm sure my Great Aunt Meredith would really appreciate that. "How environmentally kind of Robyn to give me last year's card that someone already gave to her," she'd say. It was more likely that she'd call all my relatives to tell them how tacky and cheap I was for giving her a used card. Or maybe, to ask them if I'd lost my mind and was now living in a cardboard box, rummaging in garbage cans for old Christmas cards.

I decided to stick with traditional cards, but I'd only send them to a select few out-of-town friends and relatives. I didn't want to use too much paper, but I already had three packs of Christmas cards on hand. These cards were sent to me, unsolicited, by some of the charities I support. As an environmentally conscious person, this practice drives me absolutely mental. Just because I donated fifty bucks to your worthy cause, that doesn't mean I want you to send me calendars and flashlights and monogrammed notepads with my name spelled wrong, and then expect me to pay for them! At Christmas, the charities must ramp up this negative-option giving routine. I had foot-and-mouth-painter-Christmas cards, cancer Christmas cards and heart-and-stroke Christmas cards. All of these charities expected me to pay for these cards, but I sort of felt like I already had. And if I paid again, what would they send me next? A stuffed animal? A blender? I now feel less inclined to donate money to these charities, which was obviously not their marketing department's intention.

At least Christmas lights were easy to deal with. We switched our outdoor lights to LED lights, which use up to ninety-five percent less energy. The power company was even offering rebates to customers who brought in their old-style lights. It was a no-brainer.

And there was the wrapping paper issue. I had finally run out of the Bayview fund-raising paper, and I was loath to buy more. Some of the green Christmas articles suggested wrapping gifts in pillowcases and towels. Lame! Another suggestion was to use old newspapers. When I mentioned this to my friend Trevor, he told me that his grandmother always wrapped their gifts in the funny pages.

"That's a cute idea," I said. "It's colorful and good for the environment."

"Yeah, but my grandma just did it because she was so cheap," he explained. "She also used to steal the eggs out of the pigeons' nest near her balcony and eat them."

"Oh . . . gross."

I talked to John about it. "I just won't wrap anything," I said. "The kids won't care." It was true, the kids wouldn't care. But then I thought about Christmas dinner with my mom.

My mom *loves* Christmas, with all its trimmings, trappings, and overconsumption. And she really goes for it. Christmas decorating starts on December first and takes approximately three weeks. Her house becomes a winter wonderland with nary a surface free of angels, a choir of singing mice, a light-up Christmas village, or a Nativity scene. She has fake snow and glass balls and pine boughs and holly.

I couldn't show up with unwrapped gifts. It would be sacrilegious! I could wrap them in pillowcases, but that would be even worse. I could already hear the smart remarks. My brother

Scott would say, "Oh, did you walk over here, too? It's only thirty miles." My mom would shake her head and whisper to her husband: "Couldn't she give it a rest, just at Christmas?" I'd get defensive and it would set a bad tone for the whole dinner.

But I had to do something to replace wrapping paper. I already felt guilty about my high consumption of paper products as a writer and frequent nose-blower. So I decided the gifts for my family of origin (and their kids) would be wrapped in newspaper tied with red ribbon—still fairly festive, but also environmentally friendly. There would be a few wisecracks, I was sure, but at least the eye-rolling and taunting would be kept to a minimum. I was going to do it. I was taking a stand.

Then, about a week before Christmas, I was rummaging in my closet looking for some ancient tax returns when I saw it. It had fallen down behind a stack of manila file folders: a lone, half-used roll of red-and-gold wrapping paper. That paper couldn't go to waste now, could it? I could wrap the presents, just like usual, and no one would know I'd even considered going the newspaper route. I breathed a huge sigh of relief. The pressure was off. It was a Christmas miracle!

But when it came to gifts for my kids, I wasn't sure I could compromise. Sure, the multitude of articles had green gift ideas, like a scarf you had knitted yourself out of organic wool, or a soy candle. Those just weren't going to work. I could already picture Ethan's face when he got up on Christmas morning and opened his locally made jar of organic chutney. It would not be pretty. But I had made a commitment to do Christmas green (ish) and I was going to stick to it. I needed to talk to my kids about cutting down on the usual toys and paraphernalia that accompany the holiday. As you can imagine, my suggestion was met with the requisite horror.

"I didn't say we were going to *cancel* Christmas," I explained as my kids stared at me, blinking back tears. "I just don't think we need to go overboard."

"So what does that mean?" Ethan tried to maintain his composure. "Not going overboard?"

I explained my environmental stance in gentle yet firm terms. "Toys have a lot of packaging that ends up in landfills. And you already have so many toys that you don't even play with. Why would we add to that with more toys that you'll soon grow tired of? All I'm saying is that I'm going to think about waste and the environment when I'm doing my shopping this year."

They heard: "*Blah blah blah blah* less presents."

But I vowed to do it. And while I wasn't going to have time to knit an organic scarf, surely I could think of some low-impact gifts for my kids? It was not that easy. What do kids like? Construction sets, dolls, electronics, and action figures. Plastic, plastic, and then some more plastic!

And then it occurred to me that I could give them an experience rather than an object. The kids were eager to learn to ski and snowboard, and John and I were eager for them to learn, as well. So we bought the children a week of skiing and snowboarding lessons at Grouse Mountain. I know there are environmental ramifications to downhill skiing and driving to the North Shore mountains, but it still beat buying the kids a bunch of plastic garbage. They had both been given hand-me-down equipment, which we supplemented at the consignment store. It was an excellent gift. They'd learn a fun, healthy winter activity. We'd support our local economy. And it was just a slip of paper. No wrapping paper! No packaging!

But that night, as I dropped the gift certificates into their stockings, I panicked. "They're going to be disappointed!" I cried. "I've ruined Christmas! It's like I've killed Santa Claus!" I proceeded to fill their socks with cheap chocolate bells in the hope that the sugar rush would distract from their disappointment.

To my surprise, the kids were fine. In fact, they were as happy as at any other Christmas. Of course, my "not going overboard" stance did not extend to grandparents, aunts, and uncles who continued to spoil them rotten, so I'm not sure they actually noticed a difference.

The adults in my family don't exchange gifts. You can't get any more environmentally friendly than that. Or can you? One year, my mom bought all her kids a rooster and two hens. Another year, I got my stepdad a goat. They were a little hard to wrap, but still . . . great gifts.

The livestock was for a village in Africa, not to keep in the backyard for fresh eggs and goats' milk. These charitable gifts were socially responsible as well as waste free. It's a tradition I really want to continue. And charitable giving has gotten so fun and creative. Organizations like World Vision and Plan Canada offer so many options. What better gift for a new mom (or your mom) than midwife training for women in Uganda? Or immunizations for kids in Bolivia? You can donate a pig to a family in rural China on behalf of your overweight uncle. Or

HIV care kits to Kenya for your promiscuous cousin! One Valentine's Day, I bought John honeybees for an African village. Get it? *Honey* for my honey on Valentine's Day.

So I will keep dreaming of a green Christmas. Doing the holidays sustainably can be a daunting endeavor, especially as the Christmas marketing machine revs up and I get caught up in all the hoopla. But I'm going to try to stick with it. Will I be able to think of low-impact gift ideas for my kids next year? I hope so. Am I going to break down and buy a roll of wrapping paper when the festive season comes around again? I'll really try not to. And at Christmas, I think *trying* is good enough—because if I put too much green pressure on myself at that time of year, I'm destined for a nervous breakdown . . . or a serious rum-and-eggnog addiction. If I can do Christmas green-ish, that's good enough for me. For the moment, at least.

A Green Field Trip

• • •

THE AD READ: EPIC, Vancouver's Sustainable Living Expo.

I was a living sustainably! Or at least, I was doing my best. Obviously, I had to attend.

"It will be educational for the kids," I said to John. "And maybe even for us. Though we're already doing a lot of sustainable things."

"We sure are," he agreed. "But it couldn't hurt to pick up a few more tips."

I thought this field trip would be good for Ethan, in particular. By this time, my son was what you'd call a "selective" environmentalist, teetering between zeal and indifference. While he could be extremely enthusiastic about protecting the planet, there were times when he was the farthest thing from

green. It seemed that his passion for saving the earth was stron-
gest when it worked to his advantage: like when his grandma
was serving him conventional asparagus and he refused to
eat it, but he'd suddenly forget his environmental principles
when offered conventional birthday cake. On second thought,
I think we could all be accused of this kind of "convenient"
environmentalism.

I told the kids about our plans to visit EPIC. "What kind of
stuff will they have there?" Ethan asked.

"Ummm . . . All sorts of sustainable living stuff."

My offspring looked at me, unimpressed. I couldn't blame
them, really. How interesting could sustainable living stuff
really be? I scoured the ad again for some enticing exhibits.

"They have hybrid cars!" I cried triumphantly.

"Cool!" Ethan, who loves cars, replied.

"And cooking demonstrations!"

"Yay!" Tegan, who loves food, replied.

So we headed down to the Vancouver Convention and
Exhibition Center, its fabric sails now an icon of the city. Other
than hybrid cars and chef demonstrations, I wasn't really sure
what to expect. The EPIC Web site said that the mandate of
the sustainability expo was "to bring together consumers and
producers who care about Earth-friendly, ethically sourced,
healthier products and services." Still, I didn't know what that
meant *specifically*. I just hoped it wouldn't be totally boring for
the kids . . . or the adults.

After shelling out roughly the cost of Ethan's anticipated
braces to park our car under the building, we made our way to

the exhibition space. Entering the enormous room, I was blown away by the sheer size of the event. As far as the eye could see, there were booths upon booths of green vendors. There were green wedding planners, eco-friendly contractors, organic skin-care producers, and ethical investment advisers. There were ecotour providers, green gardeners, and even "sustainable" real estate agents. And there was food, a lot of food.

We hadn't expected the Sustainable Living Expo to be a ver-itable smorgasbord of free samples, but we weren't complaining. The kids lined up for three different flavors of hard-bite potato chips, healthy because they were cooked in olive oil. Then we sampled dried tropical fruit produced by a company that employed women from a Colombian refugee camp. John and I tasted fair-trade coffee and wine that came in a box instead of a bottle. We had our first matcha tea latte and some ethically produced chocolates. Ethan and Tegan guzzled organic juices and natural sodas, greedily scarfing down healthy energy bars and organic muffins. We felt compelled to buy most of these products. We couldn't stand there pigging out on free samples and then just walk away.

I was finally able to lure my family away from the food to check out the cars. Ethan and John cheerfully inspected the hybrid Toyotas and Lexuses. They looked at the smart cars and biodiesel vehicles. Tegan and I were less intrigued. "Let's go look at the clothes," I suggested.

My daughter and I wandered over to the textiles. It was like being at the mall, except the sustainable and green mall! There were adorable kids' clothes and trendy women's fashions all made of soy, hemp, or bamboo. Of course, given that these sustainable garments weren't sewn by eight-year-olds in India, they were a little on the pricey side. Tegan picked up a gorgeous top and held it to her chest.

"Should we get it?" I asked.

"Can I?" she cried, her face lighting up.

I looked at the price tag. Eep! It was a lot more than I was used to paying for a shirt she'd grow out of in a few months. But it was so cute and sustainable and ethically sewn. It was worth the extra money.

When we had purchased the top, we continued on, stroking the bamboo towels, fingering the organic cotton bedding. We paused at a booth selling hip, reusable canvas bags. They weren't cheap but they were hip and reusable. And I had to get one to carry my daughter's new sustainable and ethical soy shirt.

Tegan insisted that we watch the upcoming eco-fashion show. I expected the guys to resist, but they were happy to sit and rest their feet (walking around with all those free samples in our stomachs was tiring). As we waited for the event to start, a slide show educated us with green tips and uplifting facts about the many ways everyday household items are killing us. Did you know that your plastic shower curtain is poisoning you? Well, it is. That plasticky smell comes from its off-gassing, hormone-disrupting chemicals (yes, potential man boobs from the shower curtain). And you were probably not aware that the mattress you sleep on has been sprayed with flame retardants and pesticides. Your sheets have been, too. Oh, and by the way, you may as well shoot yourself as you eat food fried in a nonstick pan. Those coatings are deadly! Eventually the models took to the stage and spared us from this useful but highly depressing information.

When it was over, John suggested we check out the exhibit of his employer, BC Hydro. Their booth was all about saving energy, which was obviously not as exciting as cars, clothing, or free food. But to demonstrate the efficiency of compact fluorescent lightbulbs, they had an exercise bike hooked to a CFL and a regular lightbulb. By pedaling the bike, you could see how much energy it took to light each type of bulb. When you flicked the switch to the regular lightbulb, it felt like you were pedaling up the side of a mountain. When you switched to the CFL bulb, it was like taking a leisurely cruise along the seawall. What a great demonstration!

I could not get Tegan off that thing. For some reason, she found the stationary lightbulb bike about forty times more fun than her regular bike at home. I tried to get her to move on, but she was obsessed.

"Please, Mom? Can I just ride for a few more minutes?" Flick, flick of the switch from CFL to regular lightbulb and back. "I just love this lightbulb bike. I don't know why. It's just so fun. Please? A few more seconds?"

"Okay," I acquiesced, wandering off to read some rather dull information about energy conservation. When I returned a few minutes later, I noticed that Tegan's enthusiasm had attracted other kids wanting to ride the coolest stationary bike in the history of the world. A lineup of children had formed.

"Whennnnn?" I heard a youngster whine to his mother. "When can I go on the lightbulb bike?"

"Just as soon as that girl who's been on there for twenty minutes deigns to let someone else have a turn," the mother retorted.

Tegan had hogged the lightbulb bike for long enough. It was time to step in.

As I removed my daughter from her ride, I noticed John chatting to someone. Upon further inspection, I recognized John's boss and his wife from the previous year's Christmas party. Well, wasn't this just a fortunate coincidence? Here was John, with his lovely wife and kids, checking out the BC Hydro exhibit at the sustainability expo. What a keen employee! What a great dad! Didn't we look like the perfect little green family? John was probably going to get a raise now. Or a promotion! I hoped John's boss had seen how much Tegan enjoyed the lightbulb bike.

I ran into a few other friends and acquaintances, too. Trevor was there with his partner, Keith, looking for fixtures for their green-home renovation. I wasn't surprised to bump into them. Much like us, they were making a concerted effort to live sustainably. I also saw a former coworker and her fiancé.

"Hi Megan," I said. "I didn't know you had an environmental conscience." (I didn't say the last part out loud.) Megan and I chatted briefly before continuing our browsing. As I walked away, I could almost hear her telling her fiancé, "Robyn's such a great mom. How many parents care enough about their children's environmental education and conscience to take them to the sustainability expo? Probably not that many."

Finally, we drove home full and exhausted from our after-noon at EPIC Vancouver. Despite my concerns that it might be boring, each one of us had found something to enjoy at the sus-tainability expo. But when we got home, I was a little dismayed to see how much stuff we had bought at the green event. We had toted home four bags of olive-oil potato chips, four bags of dried fruit, matcha tea powder, fair-trade coffee, the soy shirt for Tegan, the reusable canvas grocery bag, a couple of green cleaners, and a reusable dust cloth. Sure it was all Earth-friendly, ethically sourced, healthy stuff, but did we really need all of it? To add to the accumulation, I had a purse full of about thirty pamphlets on other green products and services in which I might be interested in the future.

The visit left me feeling conflicted. Was going to the sus-tainability expo just like going on a green shopping spree? Sure, that was better than going on a not-green shopping spree, but weren't there better ways to help the environment? We could have been out planting trees, weeding out invasive species, or picking up litter. Or I could have been at the Global Warming Café, discussing ways to stop climate change with a neighbor in long gray braids.

I'm torn about attending future environmental expos. It's true that we enjoyed our visit, and we did pick up some useful tips on being green. We also learned a lot about poisonous shower curtains and deadly mattresses. We now know about ethically sourced tea leaves and dried fruit and eco-vacations. But is visiting a sustainability expo really the best way to show our love for the planet? Wouldn't it be better to take a walk along the beach? Or go for a hike through the forest? Or do anything that doesn't mandate that we come home with a trunkload of unnecessary products? So maybe people like us, people who can't control their buying and sampling impulses, should steer clear of such exhibitions? Although . . . it is good for our green image to be seen at such an event. And what if John's boss is at the next one, too?

A Dirty Habit

• • •

HAD ALMOST REACHED a level of calm acceptance about my green status. Sure, I could have been greener. I could have installed solar panels on my roof and started bathing in collected rainwater. I could have launched an official opposition to the birthday-party loot bag and started a door-knocking campaign to encourage my neighbors to eat more lentils and less meat.

But look at all the good things I was doing: unplugging appliances, driving as little as possible, washing my clothes in cold water, thinking about where my food came from . . . Sure, they were just small things, but they all added up to make me a pretty darn green person. I did fall short in several areas. I still refused to ride the bus and was a fan of long, hot baths with water up to my eyebrows. I colored my hair with toxic chemicals and planned to continue until I was at least eighty, when I would suddenly, gracefully, embrace my gray. So maybe I wasn't "pretty darn green." Maybe I was just *light* green.

And for a moment, I was at peace. I didn't feel guilty or conflicted or stressed-out. Yes, I was light green—which wasn't as good as dark green, but was a lot better than not green at all. I revelled in the moment. I drank it in. And then, it was gone. That's when I remembered that I had one dirty, nasty, carbon-spewing habit that could quite possibly erase all the small green things I was doing as null, void, pointless . . . I had a chronic and serious addiction to air travel.

I met my husband in 1994 on a Greek Island. "Oh, what a romantic place to meet," you are probably thinking. Everyone thinks that until I grudgingly admit that the Greek Island we met on was Ios. If you have never heard of Ios, let me tell you that it is one of the beautiful Cyclades Islands, famous for its intense, all-night party scene. Young people from all over the world congregate there to get sunburned, get wasted, and get lucky.

I met John in one of the island's infamous nightclubs. It was about four in the morning, and I was staggering around looking for my girlfriend, who happened to be out in the alley barfing up her ouzo shots. As I passed by a table, I looked up to see a shirtless, bronzed hunk dancing on top of it. He pulled me up to dance with him, and the rest, as they say, is history. Pretty romantic, huh?

Obviously, I wasn't thinking about the logistical and environmental impact of hooking up with a guy from the other side of the globe. In fact, I thought we were just having a holiday fling that would be nothing but a happy, if somewhat hazy, memory. But somehow, it all got out of hand and the next thing I knew, he had moved to Canada, and we were married with two kids.

As I mentioned before, marrying an Australian and transplanting him to Canada necessitates a few trips Down Under. It's not like John can never see his mom again. I already feel bad enough that I stole her son from her and often worry that my karmic payback will mean one of my kids will move to Finland while the other lives in Johannesburg. It's important that we make the trip to Australia, despite the twenty-odd tons of carbon the airplane spews into the air.

It's not like we go to Perth twice a year or anything. In fact, in fourteen years together, we have only visited twice (and we just booked our third trip). A round-trip plane ticket from Vancouver to Perth costs about $2,500. For the four of us, that's ten grand. And let's not forget that the trip is twenty-three hours of flying time, with at least two stopovers. All up, the journey takes about two days (but on the way home, you actually travel back in time, so it takes about an hour). Did you know it takes your body a full day to recover for every time zone you have travelled through? On a trip to Perth, you travel through sixteen time zones. Yes, we feel like crap for sixteen days after we get home.

I don't mean to sound like a whiner. I love Perth and visiting with John's family. The expense and physical toll of the flight are well worth it. And when we fly to Australia, I don't even feel *that* bad about the carbon emissions. Because this is John's homeland we're talking about. His family! Who could begrudge an immigrant a trip home once in awhile?

So if my trips to Australia every four years were the only flights I took, I wouldn't feel guilty at all. But they're not. It pains me to admit it, but I travel as much as I can—which is not that much compared to a jet-setting socialite or a touring rock star or a professional basketball player. It's not even that much compared to a businessperson or someone involved in a bi-coastal love affair. Still, I do fly two or three times a year. It's bad, I know, but I just love to travel. I can't get enough!

I'm not sure whom to blame for my addiction to excitement and adventure. It's not like I grew up in a globe-trotting family. My parents took me to Disneyland and Maui, which was apparently enough to jump-start my love of exotic locales. When I was in twelfth grade, I travelled with my two best friends to Oahu. I worked hard pumping gas and saved up enough money to spend ten days on Waikiki beach. It was an amazing experience that taught me to never, ever let my seventeen-year-old daughter travel to a tropical party destination where there are a lot of sailors on leave.

And then, in 1994, I spent six months backpacking through Europe. It was the highlight of my life. Yeah, I know I'm supposed to say the highlight of my life was my wedding day or the birth of my children, but frankly, my wedding day was quite stressful. And giving birth is not fun. Whoever says giving birth is the highlight of their life must have been given better drugs than I was. My kids are the highlight of my life now, but come on! A trip to Europe or twelve hours in labor? That's not a tough call.

The travelling eased off for a while when the children were

young, so we weren't doing too much damage to the environment. But last year, John and I flew to South America. My friend Shawn, a wealthy Manhattan real estate agent, had invited fourteen of his closest friends to celebrate his fortieth birthday with him in a beachside town in Brazil. Búzios is a three-hour bus ride outside of Rio de Janeiro, and was made famous in the sixties when Brigitte Bardot chose it as her summer retreat. If Brigitte Bardot liked it there, I was quite certain I would, too.

Shawn had rented an eight-bedroom house complete with pool, cook, and groundskeeper. He had booked a bus to take us into Rio and secured a private box in the Sambadrome for us to watch Carnival. Yes, Carnival, the undisputed best party in the world. We were going to watch it from a private box. A *private box!* He'd also arranged tours to Sugarloaf Mountain and Christ the Redeemer on Corcovado Mountain (one of the New Seven Wonders of the World, I might add). We would visit Ipanema beach! We'd spend a night at the Copacabana Palace! My mom even offered to look after the kids and the dog.

So what was I supposed to say? "Sorry Shawn, I can't go. I feel too bad about the airplane emissions. Thanks anyway for this once-in-a-lifetime opportunity." I suppose a super, deep-dark-green person would have, but I didn't.

The following fall, I flew to Las Vegas for my birthday. I know, Vegas. The name alone is synonymous with greed, excess, waste, and debauchery. I was so excited! Ethan seemed to think he should have been invited on my birthday trip, as well.

"Vegas is for grown-ups," I told him as he attempted to guilt-trip me for ditching him.

"My friend Seth says it's his favorite holiday destination in the whole world," my son countered. "His parents take him there every year."

"Well, Seth's parents obviously have a sexless marriage and have lost their sense of fun," I said. "This trip is grown-ups only."

John was attending a conference, so I flew down to join him. Yes, I felt a twinge of green guilt as I boarded the plane. Only six months before, I'd boarded an even larger plane to jet off to South America. But I was too excited to dwell on it. It was my first time in Vegas. It was my birthday!

And once I arrived, all thoughts of pollution and energy conservation and responsible water use flew right out of my mind. I was in Vegas, baby! I cranked up the air conditioning when it was too hot. I threw my plastic water bottles in the trash when I was done with them (Vegas has no recycling facilities). I went gambling and shopping and to a spectacular show. I had a margarita at ten AM. I ate dinner at one in the morning. It was complete and utter hedonism. After all, "what happens in Vegas stays in Vegas"—including my empty water bottles, in a landfill for all eternity.

There was a solution to my flying addiction. Okay, maybe it wasn't really a *solution*, but it had to be better than nothing. I could buy carbon offset points. By supporting projects such as wind farms, solar installations, or energy-efficiency projects, I could pull carbon out of the air to make up for the carbon my flight was putting into the air. I'd heard Al Gore say that he was flying "carbon neutral," so I decided to look into it.

I googled: "carbon offset points."

Practically all the results were negative, with words like "scam" and "scheme" jumping off the screen. Apparently, there was no regulated carbon-credit system in place in Canada. And some environmentalists said that carbon offsets were actually having a negative effect. They do nothing to address the fact that air travel is the fastest-growing source of greenhouse-gas emissions in the world, and people should quit flying and take the train. Really, the plethora of online articles said, carbon offsets just make people feel better about their bad, carbon-belching habits.

But I *wanted* to feel better about my bad, carbon-belching habits. Wasn't that the point? And sure, I could take the train— but not to Australia! And this wasn't Europe, where you could travel from country to country within a few hours. This was Canada, the second-biggest country in the world. It would take me forty hours to get to Winnipeg by train—and I didn't even want to go to Winnipeg! No, giving up flying was not an option. I would have to buy the offset points for my next flight. With our massive family trip to Australia looming, I had to do something to assuage the guilt.

It wasn't an easy decision, though. While there were many offset plans to choose from, they weren't all created equal. For example, some offset plans said they took your money and used it to plant carbon-replenishing trees to counteract your flight. This sounded great, but *Ecoholic* pointed out that trees take years to mature to the point where they actually absorb significant amounts of carbon—and that's if they survive logging, windstorms, and pine beetles. Other offset plans invest

your money in renewable energy like wind, solar, or geother-
mal. And still another was supporting landfill methane projects.
Or, I could contribute to energy-efficiency projects that reduce
energy use, much of which comes from coal, oil, and natural
gas. Some offset programs would even let me choose where my
money went (like I'm an environmental scientist and know the
best way to suck carbon out of the atmosphere now?).

According to John Lee's article *Travelling Light,* in the pre-
miere issue of *Granville* magazine, you could even shop around
for the cheapest offset deal. Given the cost of our Australia trip,
that was a very sensible idea. So I checked out a few recommended programs to see what it would cost me to offset our trip
to Perth.

The first one I checked was a UK-based carbon offsetter. I
had read (in *Ecoholic*) that the travel series *Lonely Planet* was
buying carbon -redits through this program to neutralize their
travelling staff's emissions. Their site calculated the total mileage of our trip from Vancouver to Perth at 73,560 miles for the
four of us, resulting in 18.5 tons of carbon emissions. It would
cost about $281 to offset our flight.

I then went to a US Web site. According to that source, a
return flight from Vancouver to Perth produced six tons of
carbon per person, so twenty-four tons all up. But it would cost
us only $146.46 to offset our journey.

Next was a Canadian site that was the Barenaked Ladies'
choice for offsetting all their air travel. I like some of the Barenaked Ladies' music and I know they have a green conscience,
so I thought this would be a good choice. I put in our travel

details. The site told me that our Canada–Australia flight would produce total emissions of 23.2 tons. It would cost us $469 to make our trip environmentally friendly.

It was a little tough to decide. Before I automatically went the cheapest route, I decided to check out www.davidsuzuki. org. When I'm confused about environmental issues, I turn to David Suzuki, or "the Suzooks" as John and I affectionately call him. Surely the Suzooks could recommend the very best carbon offset plan out there? I went to his site, and sure enough, he did. He recommended three of them. I went to the corresponding Web pages and punched in my flight information.

The first site offered regular offsets and "Gold Standard" offsets, which are being used by several NHL players. To offset our flights to Perth with their regular carbon offsets would cost us $761.02. If we upgraded to the gold standard, it was $1,141.53! Yikes! The next site said it would cost us $1,154 to offset our flights. (That was even more than the previous one's Gold Standard!) But the next Web site informed me that we could offset our flights for just $158.40.

I was even more confused. First of all, why was there such a big cost discrepancy between the different carbon-cutting plans? Did a high price tag mean they were doing a better job sucking carbon out of the air? Or were they just premium pricing in order to attract frequent-flying rock bands and hockey teams? And why did we have to pay offset points per person? We were all on the same plane and it was going there anyway. When you think about it, shouldn't these offset companies take our body weight into account? For example, a little girl like Tegan is not weighing the plane down and causing it to use more fuel like someone the size of, say, Pavarotti. So why should Tegan have to pay the same amount as Pavarotti to offset her flight? (I know he's dead, but I couldn't think of another really famous fat man.)

I wanted to make up for my bad travelling habits, but I didn't know it was going to be so complicated . . . and expensive! I mean, I am not a professional hockey player or a Barenaked Lady (well, sometimes, but not the really rich kind). And our flights to Perth already cost a fortune. Now I had to throw in another grand to make up for the pollution?

It was only a few days after my mystifying offset research that I read a newspaper interview with several politicians talking about their travel habits. "I never fly anywhere," one politician said. "My family and I only vacation within the province, spending most of our time at Burns Lake. This cuts down on greenhouse-gas emissions and we just love Burns Lake."

I was suspicious. I mean, wasn't it possible that the politician was just *saying* she spent all her holidays at Burns Lake so voters would think she cared more about climate change than those other politicians with time-shares in Maui? But it got me thinking. I did live in one of the most beautiful places on Earth (the "best place on Earth" if you wanted to believe our license plates). Maybe I should try sticking close to home? I could visit the many beautiful sights that my province had to offer. Maybe I, too, could spend all my vacations at Burns Lake.

The notion lasted about four seconds. Forget it! No offense to Burns Lake, but there is a big, wide world out there. Would

I be content to learn the rich and varied history of Burns Lake? Would I be happy to taste the cuisine of Burns Lake? To soak in the unique culture and traditions of Burns Lake? To dance to Burns Lake's music? To admire Burns Lake's art? There was no way I could do it. Sure, I would still take vacations within British Columbia, but sometimes, I would have to get away. It was in my blood. I was a travel addict.

Since I couldn't give up flying, I would at least try to do it responsibly. I would continue to fly economy class, which is better for the environment. Because they pack more seats into the space, it's more efficient (though significantly less comfortable) than sitting in business class. And I would try to pack light—though this could be challenging depending on where I was going. I would keep myself slim and trim. I wasn't going to require the plane to use more fuel to fly my lard-ass across the ocean. And I was going to buy offset points. I just had to decide which ones.

In the end, I went with the cheapest option. Yes, the company's plan was affordable, but their site still promised to invest my money in industrial efficiency and renewable energy projects like wind farms. I know some might say that buying carbon offsets, much like a boob job or laser eye surgery, is not the time to bargain shop, but I disagree. You're about to go on a holiday. You might want that extra money to buy some souvenirs or get a pedicure. Plus, the site was endorsed by the Suzooks! And that was good enough for me.

As an added bonus, my carbon offset points came with a free green luggage tag, so I could "easily locate (my) luggage among a sea of identical bags, and advertise (my) environmental pride."

I felt kind of funny about using that luggage tag. Wasn't it kind of hypocritical to be advertising your greenness while you were flying around the world? And was it maybe just a teeny bit pious and annoying? So I decided that I would continue to offset my flights with carbon-credits but that I would leave the green tag off my suitcase. Because I know that the best thing I could do for the environment would be to stay home. Unfortunately, I just can't do that. Plus, my suitcase is red. It's not that hard to identify.

Epilogue

• • •

ONE EVENING, AS I was cooking something local and unmedicated for dinner, there was a knock at my door. As usual, my dog went mental, which, despite its constancy, always scares the heck out of me.

"Who the hell . . . ?" I said, as I stormed to answer it. This is my standard response to phone calls and knocks at the door at dinner time.

Two men were standing on my front porch. "Hi," the older of the two said, "We're with the Green Party. Could we talk to you for a couple of minutes?"

"It's not really a good time." This is my standard response to politicians who knock on my door at dinner time—or anytime, for that matter.

The younger man spoke. "I'm sorry to interrupt your evening, but I'm your delegate and I'm hoping we can count on your support in the upcoming by-election."

I paused before answering. Could the Green Party count on my support? Yes, I had been trying to be green for a couple of years now. And yes, I'd had varying degrees of success with that. I had come to accept myself as a fairly green person . . . well, green-*ish* . . . maybe a light-green person. But was I green enough to vote for the Green Party?

Here was my moment to decide, to define my level of commitment to the environment. But was I ready? It was a monumental step. Pledging my support for the Green Party meant that I cared more about protecting the environment than I did about the plethora of other social and economic issues at stake. And I did care a lot about protecting the environment. I just didn't know if I cared enough to vote Green.

Finally, I gave my ambiguous reply. "I haven't decided who I'm going to vote for yet . . . but I do care a lot about the environment."

"Great!" they chorused encouragingly.

"That's just terrific!" The older man said, "Would you be willing to put up a lawn sign saying you support the Green Party?"

A lawn sign? My brother would have a field day with that one. "I don't think so," I responded. "I don't like to advertise my political convictions."

The younger man spoke up. "Would you be willing to make a monetary contribution to the Green Party?"

"I'm right in the middle of cooking dinner here," I snapped. "I've got to go."

They handed me a flier full of highly depressing information about climate change and let me get back to the kitchen.

As the by-election grew closer, I pondered my decision. I wanted to vote for a party that put stopping climate change at the top of their priority list. Obviously, the Green Party qualified. But so did all the others! Every politician was spouting off about their passion for the environment. They all said they'd take great strides to stop global warming. So did it even matter who I voted for? If I did decide to vote Green, what did that say about me? Did it mean I was really a hippy-dippy tree-hugger? Was voting for the Green Party really just a less visible way of wearing Birkenstocks with gray wool socks?

About a week before the by-election, we happened to drive through a neighborhood full of political lawn signs. (These people obviously wouldn't be teased by their family members for advertising their political convictions.) There were a number of red Liberal Party signs, some blue Conservative Party posters, a handful of New Democratic Party banners, and one or two signs supporting the Green Party. Ethan called to us from the backseat.

"Mom . . . Dad . . . Who are you going to vote for?"

"I'm not sure yet," I admitted.

"I'm still thinking about it," John seconded.

I turned to look at my son. "Who would you vote for if you were old enough?"

"Green Party," he said confidently.

"Really?" I asked.

"Yeah . . . so they can stop global warming."

It was so simple in his ten-year-old mind. Vote Green. Stop global warming. But wasn't it more complex than that? Could a political party in Canada really halt climate change? And what about all the other issues on the table? What about homelessness and the war in Afghanistan? What about health care and the cost of post-secondary education? Did the Green Party care about all those other problems too?

That evening, I went to the Green Party's Web site (www.greenparty.ca). Yes, their site assured me, they did care about all those other problems, too. Their site said that the Green Party took a holistic approach to economic sustainability, focusing on building stronger local economies with a small-business focus; increasing national and regional self-sufficiency; providing economic diversification; expanding "fair"-trade and green-certified production; and shifting to more renewable energy. It said that Canada needed to develop a low-carbon economy, commercializing low-carbon technologies such as alternative fuels, renewable energy, and energy efficiency to reduce our reliance on fossil fuels. Their site also outlined their taxation strategy, their plans to reduce the gap between rich and poor, and their suggestions for ways to address other social inequalities.

It sounded pretty good. The Green Party was more "well-rounded" than I'd thought. But still . . . voting Green just seemed like such a radical step. I remained undecided.

As Election Day neared, the political parties ramped up their campaigning. The Liberals called to offer me a ride to the polling station (since it was at Bayview School, a block and a half away, I said I could probably make it there by myself). The NDP phoned to ask if they could count on my support. And the Green Party was everywhere! On every corner, at every bus stop, there were Green Party campaigners. They had signs and balloons and big smiles. They waved and cheered and urged me: Vote Green! Vote Green! They wanted it more than anyone. Their passion was getting to me.

The morning of the by-election, a Green Party member called me. "Can we count on your support? Please? Please? Pretty please?"

"Uh . . . oh . . . ummm . . . I think so!" I blurted. It was only a by-election after all, which meant just one seat. And if the Green Party couldn't get elected in the Vancouver Quadra riding, then where could they get elected? Probably nowhere! We should have at least one guy in the government who would put the environment first. The Green Party had done it. They had won me over with their zeal. I walked over to Bayview and cast my ballot. I voted Green.

Surprisingly, my hair didn't automatically turn gray and braid itself. I didn't hurry home and donate all my fashionable clothing to charity. And I didn't prepare an enormous lentil stew for dinner that night. Voting Green hadn't changed me at all. Or had it? Maybe voting Green had nudged me just a tiny bit farther down the color scale toward forest-green?

The Green Party didn't win; the Liberals did. The Liberal candidate had dropped a campaign leaflet through my mail slot (she had also knocked on my door, but I'd hidden in the hallway and pretended I wasn't home), which said the environment was one of her top priorities. I hoped she'd do a good job.

I was a little surprised that the Green Party had lost. It wasn't like I expected my one vote to turn the tables and give them a landslide victory, but wasn't I living in the greenest neighborhood in Canada? Why hadn't my neighbors been swayed by the party's green balloons and signs and environmental ardor? Did my community not care about the environment as much as I thought they did? And if they didn't, then why was I beating myself up about it? Why was I feeling guilty and stressed and overwhelmed with confusion? Why was I even bothering?

In the April 20, 2008, issue of the *New York Times*, Michael Pollan wrote an article with that exact title. "Why Bother?" he asked. Having read his book *The Omnivore's Dilemma*, I already knew he was going to tell me that I definitely should bother, and why. His article suggested that people "conduct themselves as if they were to live on this earth forever . . ." And if that was too daunting, to do one thing in your life that was real and particular and symbolic, to take personal environmental responsibility.

Pollan's suggestion was to plant a garden. He iterated a list of ways this would change your life for the better. You'd reduce your carbon footprint as well as your sense of dependence on the traditional, cheap-energy-based economy. You'd produce the freshest, tastiest, most local food possible, without using toxic pesticides and fertilizers. A garden would connect you with your neighbors, empower you, and provide you with fresh air and exercise.

A garden, huh? Michael Pollan obviously didn't know about

the dandelion in my front flower bed. I had walked past that weed every day for weeks. "I've got to dig that thing up," I said virtually every time I passed. "I'll find my garden tools and I'll get rid of it." Then I'd go into the house and promptly forget all about it. Sometimes, I would stop and kick at the root a few times, hoping it would magically pop out of the soil. It never did. And one day, that dandelion went to seed and blew its nasty little offspring all over the lawn. If I couldn't get it together to dig up one dandelion, how could I be expected to plant a garden? The sad fact was, I couldn't.

But last Earth Day, Tegan brought home a little sapling she'd been given at school. "Can we plant it in the backyard?" she asked eagerly.

"Of course," I replied, digging through the cupboard for my long-neglected garden tools. We went into the backyard and planted the tiny spruce. It wasn't a garden, but at least it was something.

So maybe I hadn't become the deep-dark-green goddess I'd hoped to be. But still, I was going to do my best; I was going to bother. I would bother to do all the small things I could in my own life to be low impact, sustainable, and environmentally friendly. I would continue to sign petitions to protect the boreal forest and donate money to save the habitat of obscure bears. I'd recycle and unplug appliances and walk whenever I could. And the most important thing I would do for the environment was to raise two kids who cared about trees and animals and people and the earth. And one day, maybe they'd reach that pinnacle of greenness that I could never quite achieve.

My kids may look back on their childhood and feel disappointed that their mother didn't do a better job at living a sustainable life. They may think I was confused and uninformed and downright lazy. But at least they won't look back on their childhood and say: "My mom was very very green. She was a super-sustainable eco-mom! And then one day, they carted her off to the loony bin."